THE PRAYER ADVENTURE

THE PRAYER ADVENTURE

*An anthology
compiled by Jean Watson*

HIGHLAND BOOKS

'Scripture quotations in this publication are from
the Holy Bible, New International Version.
Copyright © 1973, 1978, 1984 International Bible
Society. Published by Hodder & Stoughton.'

ISBN 0 946616 50 7

Printed in Great Britain for
HIGHLAND BOOKS
Broadway House, The Broadway
Crowborough, East Sussex TN6 1BY
by Richard Clay (the Chaucer Press) Ltd.,
Bungay, Suffolk.
Typeset by CST, Eastbourne.

CONTENTS

INTRODUCTION

Is prayer 'a little talk with Jesus'? Or believing 'six impossible things before breakfast'? It can be. It can also be listening to God; receiving from him the faith to believe 'impossible things' and the strength to attempt them; practising the presence of God throughout the day. In choosing the extracts in this anthology, I have had in mind that prayer, being a relationship between God and us, can involve any aspect of his nature and life and ours. You can't get much richer or broader than that.

I have also gone for quotes that stated old truths memorably or brought 'new' truths to my notice. For me, the test of truth is the Bible—hence the biblical basis throughout, for which I am very grateful to Hodder and Stoughton, since it is their New International Version that I have used.

While working on this book, I asked many people to lend me their books about prayer. One person replied that he had very few books about prayer, adding, with a smile, 'If I read books about prayer, I don't think I would have time to pray!' He had a point. (The same could apply to compiling books about prayer!) But my hope is that all who dip into this anthology will be spurred on, in their prayer adventure, to pray more often, more wholeheartedly and more effectively.

Jean Watson

1

The Range of Prayer
(All human life is here)
Part I

Adoring God

I am my lover's and my lover is mine.

Song of Songs 6:3

Mary took about a pint of pure nard, an expensive perfume; she poured it on Jesus' feet and wiped his feet with her hair. And the house was filled with the fragrance of the perfume.

John 12:3

I love the Lord, for he heard my voice; he heard my cry for mercy.

Psalm 116:1

What is Christian adoration? It is far more than contemplating or admiring God. It is the kneeling down of our innermost spirit in deepest awe and solemn loyalty before God, conscious of the unspeakable difference between us, the creatures, and God, the creator; between our darkness and his light, our sin and his purity, our lostness and his mercy, our nothingness and his all. Something of this sense of contrast underlies all true adoration.

Adoration looks with true joy to the Holy One, but it never forgets that it looks *up*. It rejoices in God but its joy is penetrated with the consciousness of surrender: I said to the Lord, 'You are my Lord; apart from you I have no good thing' (Psalm 16:2).

In preparing for adoration, Bible study is vital, for in Scripture is inexhaustible matter for adoration: God's creatorship; his sovereignty; his holiness; his love. The Scriptures are full of aids to adoration because their centre is God, their theme is his glory and they bless us by revealing to us God in Christ. To study the Scriptures in this way, we must give ourselves time and renounce the spirit of hurry altogether.

Adoration chastens and uplifts us; it deepens our peace with and in God; it helps us to focus not on ourselves but on God and others.   *H. C. G. Moule*

When we begin our prayers with adoration, we are setting the tone for our coming to God in confession, in thanksgiving and in supplication.

R. C. Sproul[1]

Praising and Worshipping God

Through Jesus ... let us continually offer to God a sacrifice of praise—the fruit of lips that confess his name.   **Hebrews 13:15**

Praise the Lord, O my soul; all my inmost being, praise

his holy name. Psalm 103:1

Come, let us bow down in worship, let us kneel before the Lord our Maker. Psalm 95:6

Offer your bodies as living sacrifices, holy and pleasing to God—which is your spiritual worship.
Romans 12:1

Honour God with your body. 1 Corinthians 6:20

In the ear of God everything he created makes exquisite music, and man joined in the paean of praise until he fell. Then there came the frantic discord of sin. The realisation of redemption brings man by way of the minor note of repentance back into tune with praise again.

Oswald Chambers

Increasingly the joy of creation will inspire us to praise: the first buds of spring on the trees; the first few flowers after winter; the kaleidoscope of colours in the trees of autumn; the magnificence of a sunset; the delicacy of frost on the window; the contours of the mountains, lakes and forests; the rich variety of animal life; the miracles of birth and growth; the resources of the earth; the ability to create and invent; life itself in all its fullness. Think of the Creator and enter the wide arena of praise!

Michael Baughen[2]

Praise can transform your daily life. Praise can transform your prayer life. Praise can speed victory in your prayer battles. There is no substitute for praise. Praise honours God, brings joy to the angels and strikes terror in any evil spirits who may be around. Praise clears the atmosphere, washes your spirit, multiplies your faith and clothes you with God's presence and power.

Wesley Duewel[3]

Praise is closely linked to worship because it is a verbal expression of our adoration. The difference between praise and thanksgiving that I would like to draw is that the first is our response to God who is, whereas the latter is our response to what he has done.

Ken Gardiner[4]

How can we worship in prayer? By reflecting first on who God is and thanking him for the things he has revealed about himself. To worship in prayer is to allow our spirits to feast on what God has revealed concerning his acts in the distant and recent past and what he has told us about himself. Slowly, as we review these things in a spirit of thanksgiving and recognition, we can sense our spirits beginning to expand, to take in the broader reality of God's presence and being. Slowly our consciousness is able to accept the fact that the universe about us is not closed or limited, but is in fact as expansive as the Creator meant it to be. As we enter into worship, we remind ourselves of how great he is.

Gordon Macdonald[5]

There's more to knowing God and thus more to worship than an intellectual understanding of God's words. We can't fully worship God when we ignore half of his nature. He creates, he shows imagination; he calls for the same thing in us. Awe, wonder, excitement. When was the last time we felt any of those things about our world? Most of the time, we complain.

The purpose of living with imagination, of changing how you see life, is to become worship, to learn how to worship perpetually with whatever you do or say.

Service and worship are inseparable. Worship is a service of praise and adoration, a recognition of priorities. The acts of worship, whether formal or informal, whether through singing hymns or doing our best, say that we know who is first, who's in charge, who's the boss. That is why we can't relegate worship to a once-a-week habit. We keep wanting to be the boss; our ambitions constantly get in the way. Only by living in worship will we get away from promoting ourselves to head man.

Cheryl Forbes[6]

If we truly appreciate just who God is, this will affect every aspect of our lives. We will recognise that our possessions are not truly ours at all. We will use them, including our money, to bring glory to God. That is worship. We will appreciate in a new way just how selfish or arrogant we have been and we will beg God to forgive us. That is worship. We will long that others should see the same truth about God that we have seen and we will seek to bring them to acknowledge his rule also. That is worship. Our hearts will overflow with gratitude that he, who is so great and holy, loves us so much and we will express our thanks both in words (thanksgiving) and in what we do (service). That is worship.

Ken Gardiner[7]

If you turn to Psalm 150, you'll see that it's a list of encouragements to praise, to use instruments and voices and to dance. David danced before the Lord in worship, and Isaiah and many of the prophets fell flat on their faces before the majesty of God. Others bowed and many raised their arms and hands to the Lord. The worship of the heart showed itself in the placing and movement of the body. As their bodies worshipped, so God's people worshipped.

We see several instances of worship in the Bible which are possible to act out for ourselves. Mary poured her expensive ointment over the feet of Jesus. Kneel down, cup your hands and gently offer and spill out your praise to him. At first, Mary did not recognise Jesus when God raised him from the dead, but he called her by name and she knew and turned to him then. Imagine Jesus using your name, calling to you gently and reassuringly. Turn to him; look into his face, and tell him you love him. Thomas refused to believe that his Lord was alive until Jesus invited him to touch his wounds. His response then was, 'My Lord and my God.' Be Thomas, touch Jesus and then, if you wish, fall at his feet in front of him. He may lead you to bow before him or to sit at his feet.

Rosemary Budd[8]

Thanking God

Let us come before him with thanksgiving.   Psalm 95:2

I will praise God's name in song and glorify him with thanksgiving.   Psalm 69:30

I thank Christ Jesus our Lord, who has given me strength, that he considered me faithful, appointing me to his service. 1 Timothy 1:12

Sing and make music in your heart to the Lord, always giving thanks to God the Father for everything in the name of our Lord Jesus Christ. Ephesians 5:19, 20

When we ask 'grace before meat' let us remember that it is not to be a mere pious custom but a real reception of the idea of Jesus that God enables us to receive our daily bread from him.

Oswald Chambers

Thanksgiving . . . brings joy and gratitude within. Sometimes when the heart is dry and unfeeling, reason and grace drive us to cry aloud to our Lord, recalling his passion and great goodness. And the strength of our Lord's word comes to the soul and fires the heart, and leads it by grace into its real business, enabling it to pray happily and to enjoy our Lord in truth.

Julian of Norwich

Sometimes, perhaps tonight, try spending half an hour thanking God. Thank him for himself; think of all the attributes of God—such as his majesty, power, love, holiness; his creation in all its vastness, yet his love for you individually; enter into the experiences of Abraham and thank him for providing a substitute for Isaac; thank him for his long patience in forbearing judgment on the children of Israel despite their continuous insubordination and churlishness; then thank him for his patience with you. Thank him for sending Elijah and the prophets. Thank him for sending the Lord Jesus; for the blind man who was healed, the leper who was cleansed; for stilling the storm and strengthening the disciples' faith—and yours.

Begin as far back as you can remember and thank him for the way he has protected you when you came near to accident or death; for your parents; your educational opportunities; your career; your family; assurance of his continued leading in the future, come life or death; thank him for the heavenly home he is even now preparing for you. And if you can't think of anything more, while on your knees, open your Bible to the psalms and read one prayerfully.

Kenneth N. Taylor[9]

An especially meaningful goal of thanksgiving is to thank God each day for at least one blessing you cannot remember thanking him for previously. This will require a moment of quiet contemplation concerning God's goodness.

In seeking a point of focus for this type of thanksgiving, you may wish to look at past experiences. Perhaps God granted you a specific favour or some particular blessing decades ago for which you never expressed thanks.

Do you recall ever thanking God specifically for the person who first told you about Jesus? Have you thanked God for your first Bible or for the Sunday School teacher who encouraged you in your early years of faith?

D. Eastman[10]

Thanksgiving is a lifestyle ... Long before he answers, God requires an attitude of thanksgiving.

Our ultimate goal is to be engulfed by, saturated with and completely controlled by an attitude of gratitude. Not some emotional high or an escape from reality, but the actual living in a state of thankfulness—before, during and after we receive answers to our prayers.

Evelyn Christenson[11]

Confessing to God

Father, I have sinned against heaven and against you. I am no longer worthy to be called your son. Luke 15:21

O Lord, have mercy on me; heal me, for I have sinned against you. Psalm 41:4

You cannot deal with sin until you look at it in the eye. Undress it. Strip off the jacket of excuses you made to cover its ugliness. Tear away shirts, pants, everything that hides its nakedness, then say, 'This is my child. I, and I alone, am responsible for it.' Look in your mirror, too. The person staring back at you is quite capable of committing the same sin tomorrow. Tell that person so. Don't pull any punches. Say kindly but firmly that this is the sort of thing that person is all too capable of and until he wakes up to that fact progress in godliness is impossible.

John White[12]

Confession is a heartfelt recognition of what we are. It is important to God because it indicates that we take seriously our mistakes and failures. Of course, God does not ask us to confess our sins because *he* needs to know that we have sinned, but because he knows that *we* need to know that we have sinned.

D. Eastman[13]

When I first began to follow Christ seriously, he pointed out many major behaviour and attitude patterns that, like boulders, had to be removed. And as the years went by, many of these great big boulders did indeed get removed. But when they began to disappear, I discovered a whole new layer of action and attitude in my life that I had not previously seen. But Christ saw them and rebuked them one by one. The removal process began again. Then I reached that point in my Christian life where Christ and I were dealing with stones and pebbles. They were too numerous to imagine and, as far as I can see, for the rest of my days on earth I will be working with the many stones and pebbles in my life.

Gordon Macdonald[14]

In opening ourselves to the gaze of God, we must be prepared to deal with specific sins. A generalised confession may save us from humiliation and shame but it will not ignite inner healing. In our confession we bring definite sins: the sins of heart —pride, avarice, anger, fear—as well as the sins of the flesh—sloth, gluttony, lust, murder.

Sorrow as it relates to confession is not primarily an emotion, though emotion may be involved. It is an abhorrence of having committed the sin, a deep regret at having offended the heart of the Father. Sorrow is an issue of the will before it is an issue of the emotions. In fact, being sorrowful in the emotions without a godly sorrow in the will destroys the confession. Sorrow is a way of taking confession seriously.

A determination to avoid sin is the third essential for a good confession. We ask God to give us a yearning for holy living, a hatred for unholy living.
Richard Foster[15]

Self-examination is not identical with confession but it is vitally connected with it. I do plead for careful, thoughtful, unhurried, unreserved self-examination done in the full searchlight of Scripture. Such self-examination will not be morbidly introspective; it will be severe but healthy.

Have there been any hard, censorious thoughts towards others or any needless, loveless, critical talk about them? Has there been any difference with a friend or brother, in which we have loved self, perhaps under the guise of being zealous for God? Has there been pride, or vanity, or the diseased ache of jealousy or envy as another's name has been warmly praised in our ears? Have we been self-indulgent? Have we given trouble where we might have saved or taken it? Have we trifled with truth? Have we been ashamed of the name of Jesus Christ and more anxious to stand well with society than to be true to him? Have we failed to serve our Master?

Confess it all to our eternal High Priest. Totally renounce and repudiate the things confessed and ask for cleansing and deliverance. Without renunciation and self-surrender and, where relevant, reparation, confession is meaningless.

Like Daniel (Daniel 9:20), let us also confess before God the sins of others: of our friends and of the church; of our society and country.

H. C. G. Moule

Sharing Needs and Feelings with God

You know when I sit and when I rise; you perceive my thoughts from afar. You discern my going out and my lying down; you are familiar with all my ways.

Psalm 139:2,3

The Lord said, 'I have indeed seen the misery of my people in Egypt. I have heard them crying out because of their slave drivers, and I am concerned about their suffering. So I have come down to rescue them . . .'

Exodus 3:7,8

In all their distress he too was distressed, and the angel of his presence saved them. **Isaiah 63:9**

Do not be anxious about anything, but in everything, by prayer and petition, with thanksgiving, present your requests to God. **Philippians 4:6**

Cast all your anxiety on him because he cares for you.

1 Peter 5:7

Cares and worries

The Lord won't force you to give him the burden of your cares, your tools, your work, your life. He is always present at your side, waiting patiently and discreetly for you to give him your difficulties, but of your own accord. He's waiting for you to confide your work into his keeping. Why do you insist on keeping back so much of your work for yourself? Why do you struggle on alone and just ask God to help you? Why don't you give everything to him and let him carry your load? Why don't you give him your heart and your hands so that he can make use of them in his way?

Michel Quoist[16]

If you make up your mind not to keep back for even a moment one single worry, and thus to give everything immediately into the Lord's keeping, you will experience what it is to be strong with the very strength of God . . . Take your problem as it is and offer it to the Lord without any reservations together with the anxiety that it's causing you. How am I going to do it? How am I going to get out of this spot? What path should I take? Confidently give it all into the Lord's keeping: your uncertainty, your fear, your humiliation, the reactions of your acquaintances, what people are saying and what they will say . . .

Each night you must die to all your worries and cares, whether they are legitimate or not. In a spirit of humility, place everything in the Father's hands so that each morning he may call you from sleep to a new day—a day free from all the anxieties of yesterday . . . If you want to be free, young in spirit, joyous, peaceful, strong and successful, each day, each minute, 'cast all your anxiety on him because he cares for you' (1 Peter 5:7).

Michel Quoist[17]

We do not have to pretend to God. He knows all about us anyway. He simply wants us to share every part of our lives with him, and that includes our fears and failings, our moods and emotions, our thoughts and anxieties—everything, even those things of which we are deeply ashamed. Read the psalms and see the total honesty of the psalmist.

So it was with Jesus. We see no stoicism in the Garden of Gethsemane. He shrank from the appalling ordeal of the cross, even though he submitted himself perfectly to the Father's will.

Do not be afraid of bringing your most secret thoughts and desires to God. As soon as we are open with him, he will work gently in our lives to mould us more into the likeness of Christ.

David Watson[18]

Pain—past and present

In answer to the sufferer's cry, 'Where are you, God?' God teaches a name, the name Immanuel. When it comes to the problem of pain, the Lord is much more than a God who watches over us. He more than sympathises; he becomes involved . . .

Where is God when it hurts? He dwells with us from the beginning to the end, as the Silent Sufferer, and throughout he bears all the violent attacks of destructiveness in his own heart. God is closer to our suffering and its agony that we are ourselves.

Charles Ohlrich[19]

The other gods were strong, but thou wast
    weak;
They rode, but thou didst stumble to a throne;
But to our wounds only God's wounds can
    speak,
And not a god has wounds, but thou alone.

Edward Shillito

Our attitude towards suffering should not be one of gloomy submission or passive resignation and, most of all, it should not be one in which we affirm suffering as being good. Good can and will come of our experience of suffering but this does not mean we should venerate suffering itself as good.

Indeed our imitation of God should lead us to hate suffering as an enemy, not welcome it as a friend. Look at Jesus. He unequivocally declared war on all suffering, disease and death. He hated to see people suffer and healed all that were brought to him.

Because God works to fight suffering, so should we—vigorously. We should use every means at our disposal to combat suffering—prayer, medicine, social action, relief work and so on.

Charles Ohlrich[20]

The memory of hurts done to us in the past can . . . become obstacles in our journey towards God . . . We need to pray over these memories in order to be released from the stifling effect they are having on our lives, whether they have suddenly come into consciousness or have always been there. Imaginative contemplation on the Gospel's healing miracles are useful for this purpose. Be there in imagination at the healing, then approach Christ and ask healing for your own hurt, ailment or handicap. Through the medium of the Gospel passage you are encountering the living Christ now.

Past hurts can go very deep so do not be surprised if, having prayed for healing from the heart, having managed to forgive those concerned and experienced peace and freedom, the pain of the hurt should return later. It takes time for the bitterness and hurt to be drawn from the deeper levels of our mind and heart.

If contemplating a Gospel passage does not help you to face the bitterness and hurt, then imagine you are in a room by yourself and there is a knock at the door (Revelation 3:20) ... In imagination, take Christ on a tour of the house which is your life. Take him into those rooms, that is, those events, in which you experienced great pain and introduce him to the people who caused it. Express to them ... and to Christ the hurt you still feel and then look at him and see how he reacts to the people concerned. Do not force yourself into insincere gestures or words of forgiveness but rather let him draw the feelings and words out of you. Even if you can only say, 'I want to want to be able to forgive,' that is progress. In the same way you can ask forgiveness of those you have offended.

Gerard W. Hughes[21]

All and any needs

A sinner, and even the greatest of sinners ... should treat with God of his sad state in order to become converted; the man of bad will should converse with God precisely about his bad will in order to be delivered from it. The soul buffeted by trials should pray the prayer of the tried soul that humbles and subjects itself under the hand of God in order to recover peace.

Lehodey

What sort of things is it right to ask for? Certain things we know it is God's will that we should pray for and have, such as grace to overcome temptations, to love our neighbour, to serve God faithfully. All such we are to pray for without conditions, nothing doubting but that he will grant them. Some other things are not so clear, yet we should pray for them hopefully and persistently according to God's will.

But what about material things—for instance, praying for rain? Is God going to alter the universe for us? Surely here too our Lord's teaching is clear. Whatever precisely he meant when he told his disciples that if they had sufficient faith they could bid a mountain be cast into the sea and it would be done, he did at least mean that no material obstacles would prevent God from answering the prayer of faith. It leads us all back to the child with its father, saying everything in its heart but trusting implicitly in his love and wisdom. In this spirit we may and should ask for anything that seems of importance to ourselves.

H. Northcott[22]

Are there things about God or the Bible that trouble you? Are you upset over the injustices and hypocrisies of those around you? God cares. He wants you to share these things with him. As you do so you will begin to marvel at an infinite God who is concerned with your petty problems and who does not dismiss them as petty. Because they are important to you, they are to him too.

As for your personal requests, he has already anticipated them. He is waiting for you to make them. You do not have to twist his arm. I personally wait eagerly for my children to come to me to ask me for their allowances or to request me to read a story. When they fail to ask, I am disappointed. God has, unknown to you, been encouraging you to make some requests before you ever began to formulate them in your mind. And as for other requests which it would be wrong of him to grant you, he is only too happy that you have the confidence to be frank about them.

John White[23]

Prayer for our own needs can be an act of discipleship. The psalmist makes this clear. 'Let the morning bring me word of your unfailing love, for I have put my trust in you' (Psalm 143:8). In the midst of his problems, this man of faith declares his dependence on God's help.

David A. Hubbard[24]

Jesus told us to ask our heavenly Father to supply all our needs—physical ('Give us each day our daily bread'), spiritual ('Forgive us our sins') and moral ('Deliver us from the evil one'—Matthew 6:9–13; Luke 11:2–4); and St Paul wrote: 'In everything, by prayer and petition . . . present your requests to God' (Philippians 4:6).

John R. W. Stott[25]

To accept the things that cannot be changed requires serenity, and to change the things that can be changed requires courage; but how are we to know the difference between the two situations? We may not find it easy to decide; and that is why we ask for a third quality: wisdom. God-given serenity and God-given courage are not sufficient without God-given wisdom . . . And [James] encourages us to pray for it (James 3:17; 1:5).

Frank Colquhoun[26]

Interceding with God

I pray that out of his glorious riches he may strengthen you with power through his Spirit in your inner being, so that Christ may dwell in your hearts through faith. And I pray that you, being rooted and established in love, may have power, together with all saints, to grasp how wide and long and high and deep is the love of Christ, and to know this love that surpasses knowledge —that you may be filled to the measure of all the fulness of God.   **Ephesians 3:16–19**

Is any of you in trouble? He should pray. Is anyone happy? Let him sing songs of praise. Is any one of you sick? He should call the elders of the church to pray over him and anoint him with oil in the name of the Lord.   **James 5:13, 14**

I urge ... that requests, prayers, intercession and thanksgiving be made for everyone—for kings and all those in authority, that we may live peaceful and quiet lives in all godliness and holiness.   **1 Timothy 2:1, 2**

Remember those in prison as if you were their fellow prisoners, and those who are ill-treated as if you your- selves were suffering.   **Hebrews 13:3**

Love your enemies and pray for those who persecute you.   **Matthew 5:44**

Scripture calls us to pray for many things: for all saints; for all people; for kings and all rulers; for all who are in adversity; for the sending out of workers; for those who labour in the gospel; for all converts; for believers who have fallen into sin; for one another in our own immediate circles.

Andrew Murray

The prayer of intercession calls for intelligence, understanding, watchfulness, as well as for sympathy, intensity and sacrifice. There is often a severe discipline of patience and faith. Sometimes the answer comes immediately and sometimes it tarries. The one truth on which faith rests is that it comes.

Samuel Chadwick

Intercession is the natural expression of a life filled to overflowing with the love of God ... Jesus taught that we should love one another in the same manner as he has loved us (John 13:34–35). Christ expresses his love by living evermore to make intercession for us. If we are to love in his way, intercession must become a priority in our lives. This means that the level of our intercession is one measure of our loving.

Tim Pain[27]

The prayer of Solomon at the dedication of the temple gives a lucid and powerful view of prayer. Individual sins, national calamities, sickness, exile, famine, war, pestilence, mildew, drought, insects, damage to crops, whatever affects farming, enemies—they are all in this prayer and all are suitable for prayer.

God heard this prayer of Solomon and committed himself to undertake, to relieve, to remedy. He will always relieve, answer and bless if people pray from the heart and give themselves to real, true praying.

E. M. Bounds

Intercession of any kind is setting ourselves along-side God against the powers of evil—against all deadness and disintegration and despair—and, like all coming to grips with evil, it is bound to be costly if it is to be effective. The cross shows us that the cutting edge of prayer lies in sacrifice . . . I believe it to be true that if I am really praying for some-body I must accompany that prayer by some per-sonal sacrifice or discipline or at the least by a really concentrated urgent effort to be 'with' the person I am praying for, and, as it were, offer myself as a channel through which the love and power of God can pour into and around him.

Gonville ffrench-Beytagh[28]

The prayer of Saint Francis takes a realistic view of the world in which we live.

Lord make us instruments of thy peace. Where there is hatred, let us sow love; where there is injury, pardon; where there is discord, union; where there is doubt, faith; where there is despair, hope; where there is darkness, light; where there is sadness, joy.

It is a world where there is hatred: bitterness, strife, bloodshed; a world where people suffer injury through injustice and oppression; a world where discord reigns within families, communities, churches, nations; a world where doubt of God's love and mercy and very existence leads to despair, the despair of those for whom life has no meaning, no purpose, no future; so there is darkness of the mind and spirit and, with it, sadness of heart.

In such a situation, we pray that the Lord may

make us instruments of his peace. We are asking him to use us in a ministry of compassion and healing, of reconciliation and renewal, of encouragement and consolation. We can exercise such a ministry only by being his instruments and bringing into the life of mankind the positive qualities detailed in the prayer. And the first and greatest of these is love.

Frank Colquhoun[29]

Praying for missionary work is asking God that his own desire to draw people from every ethnic group around the world to himself might become a reality. This is his plan for our world—a multi-racial people redeemed by Christ and living for the glory of God. This is the one and only plan that will truly unite the nations and cross the barriers erected by man in his sin and folly. Prayer is therefore one of the greatest contributions we can make to worldwide peace and racial harmony, especially if we are focusing our prayers on the growth of the universal church. For the church is called to model God's pattern for living to the world. It is meant to be a constant challenge to others of what is possible by the grace of God.

John Wallis[30]

Intercessory prayer goes out to the Lord and asks him in his own way to act in the lives of others. Paul prayed that the Spirit might so work in the Ephesian Christians that Christ would dwell in their hearts through faith and that they would be filled with all the fullness of God (Ephesians 3:14–19).

At the same time, intercessory prayer brings blessing on the person praying. Henry Martyn found that in times of spiritual dryness and depression, praying for others brought him renewal.

Intercessory prayer is a deeply practical acknowledgment that to God all hearts are open; that he holds the key of all wills and lives; that he can make everything work together for his glory and our good in Jesus Christ.

Such prayer witnesses to the Christian's union with Christ; and living oneness with the heavenly Intercessor is a strong encouragement to our intercession. It also witnesses to our union with our brothers and sisters in Christ and with everyone else as potentially such.

Some great permanent subjects for intercession are the world, the church, the country, the home, the school . . . If we are asked by individual friends to remember them in prayer, let's turn this into definite prayer to God. Intercessory prayer must also enter into the work which we do for others in and for the Lord.

Let's be like Epaphras 'always wrestling in prayer' that the Colossian Christians might 'stand firm in all the will of God, mature and fully assured' (Colossians 4:12). Or like Paul in prison praying for his converts, individually, in intense and tender detail (Philemon 4).

H. C. G. Moule

Imagination has an important role to play as we pray for others . . . Having established the particular responsibility we have for our missionary representatives, the way we fulfil it in prayer is to use our imagination.

Put yourself in the place of someone in their first term of service, struggling to learn an unfamiliar language, and having to worship on a Sunday in a language which they don't really understand. Now when we use our imagination like that, we begin to pray intelligently and specifically for our friend: for patience, endurance, stickability, deliverance from despondency, a retentive memory.

Think too of what it must be like living in a different culture with new customs, a draining climate and the inevitable tensions of both emotional and physical tiredness. Relationships can become fragile on account of tiredness and the pressures of living in a close community . . . As we put ourselves imaginatively into this situation, we pray that our friends may sleep well, that they won't allow little things to become big things, that they will love one another, that they will be helped to laugh at things that might otherwise give rise to an explosion of feeling and that they might be able to shrug off tendencies to self-pity.

Derek Prime[31]

Certainly we cannot use a prayer-list as though it were a telephone directory and just run our eye down a list of names. Nor is it much better, I think, to speak the names aloud, if it is all done at speed. There is more in it than that. Wait before God in quietness. Recollect his presence, his power and his love. Wait . . .

Take a name from your list. See the person in your mind's eye. See him (or her) vividly. Gaze at him with the steady directness you might hesitate to use if you were actually face to face. Let your mind play over his circumstances and concentrate on his particular need. If it is sickness, don't wallow in the pain and other distressing details. Recognise the symptoms but don't aim to 'reproduce' them in your own feelings. Constantly doing that out of misguided sympathy and with a long list of sick people, will make you ill yourself.

Now—with his face and need vividly in mind— think of God. Think strongly. Think of God in his power and will to meet your friend's need. See your friend now (and soak in the thought) as God could make him: holy, healthy, able to meet his situation, master of the mould of circumstances in which he finds himself . . .

Now fuse the two images. Your friend in his need: God in his power and love. Hold them together in the crucible of your desiring heart . . . and you can almost feel the blessing going over.

It takes time, of course. That is why prayer lists can't be too long. That is why one ought never to ask lightly for someone else's prayers. People sometimes ask for one's prayers quite casually and with no particular need in mind. Nor do they live in expectation of any special blessing afterwards. Perhaps it was just a bit of pious patter.

Yet the great intercessors remain the men and women of secret influence in all communities, and to be mentioned in their prayers is incomparably more enriching than to be mentioned in their wills.

W. E. Sangster[32]

Our intercession must be extensive enough to sweep regularly across the whole scene displayed by the news media like the revolving scanner on a radar scope, discovering the presence of obstacles to the progress of the kingdom of God. Then we must face these mountains as Jesus told us and command them in prayer to move into the sea. The prophets speak of the strongholds of satanic power as mountains which oppose the progress of God's kingdom and encourage us to clear those mountains from the King's highway by prayer (Isaiah 41:14–15).

Social injustice and cultural evil are deeply rooted in the exaltation of bad leadership. This leadership clings to power and will not be dislodged unless the hand of God is moved to cast the mighty from their thrones and exalt the humble, the righteous leaders who are crowded into corners under the oppression of the strong.

We have the right of declaring war in prayer against every leader on earth who violates the will of God by oppressing the poor, denying civil rights and deforming society. Wherever we see satanic structures, it is our responsibility to take arms against them in prayer (2 Corinthians 10:4).

Richard Lovelace[33]

The best example, other than Jesus, of praying for our enemies is that of Stephen. After he had prayed, 'Lord Jesus, receive my spirit,' he knelt down and cried out, 'Lord, do not hold this sin against them' (Acts 7:59, 60).

H. More, T. Cadell

How do I pray for my enemy?

First, find out why he is an enemy. This will mean going out to meet him and hearing what he has against you. By doing this you may discover hurts you never knew existed. Anger is often turned into compassion when we know the reason why a person hates or despises us.

Secondly, knowing where his hurt lies, even

when he is mistaken, you can lovingly hold him before the throne of God in a more meaningful way.

Thirdly, as you pray for him with love and depth, expect God to work the miracle of change within his heart and yours and so you will receive him or her as a brother or sister.

Gary Strong[34]

I have always pictured myself when I pray as coming before the throne and facing God, so to speak: looking towards him. This attitude is surely right when we make our confession or bow before him in adoration, praise and thanksgiving. It also has a place, initially, with regard to intercession. We need to come before him as we present our petitions and share with him as we seek to discover his will.

However, once we are in the position of understanding what his will is and believing we have received our petition, then, to use picture language, we have to turn so that we stand alongside God and face towards the object of our prayers. From this position we proclaim or command that what we have requested (and obtained) be fulfilled, made real, on earth. I suppose that this final stage might not be 'prayer' as we usually understand it. Nevertheless I am now convinced that our work of intercession is not complete without it. In his ministry Jesus both taught and illustrated this principle . . .

So often when we intercede we put God between us and the need. We pray to him and ask him to act for us. Whereas God desires that once we have understood what his will is, we stand between him and the need. That is to say, he asks us to act for him. We ask him to heal the sick, whereas he says, 'You heal them by my power in you.' He sent his disciples out to preach the kingdom and to heal the sick; he did not say, 'Ask me to preach and ask me to heal.' The power is his and he must have all the glory but that power is in us. God works on earth through man.

Ken Gardiner[35]

Surrendering to God

Offer yourselves to God, as those who have been brought from death to life; and offer the parts of your body to him as instruments of righteousness.

Romans 6:13

Our surrender ought to be an entire leaving of ourselves in the hands of God, forgetting ourselves in a great measure and thinking of God only. Surrender consists in a continual forsaking and losing all self-will in the will of God; forgetting what is past, giving up the time present to God and leaving to his providence that which is to come.

Madame Guyon

The more practised I became in finding the still point before God where I could taste his love and feel his warmth, the more I longed to surrender every part of my being to him. And so I would make a conscious attempt to hand back to God all that I am, all that I possess, all that I do and all that I feel. I would echo the prayer James Borst uses: 'Take me and all I have, and do with me whatever you will. Send me where you will. Use me as you will. I surrender myself and all I possess absolutely and entirely, unconditionally and forever, to your control.'

Joyce Huggett[36]

We are called to perpetual self-consecration. We are saved to serve.

Ask God what it means, in your individual case, to acknowledge the fact that every hour and minute of the new day belongs to him, because you belong to him; what it means, for you, to acknowledge the fact that your possessions, position, abilities, knowledge, influence belong to him. Confess to him that you are his and that in this or that matter which is deeply personal to you, you do, in his name and by his Spirit, yield yourself to him.

You could say something like: 'For the whole course of this day, every hour, every minute, I own myself your personal property. I give you, for it is yours, my time, position, needs, resources, tongue, imagination, will, spirit, soul and body. You know my path: my cares and joys, my tasks and opportunities, my home, my circle, my work and calling. And in these things now specially, as long as they are your will for me, I yield myself to you.'

Don't wait for special consecration meetings to give yourself to God; let every time of prayer be a meeting between servant and master. It will be a joy to go out, day by day, from such an interview, to live out your renewed allegiance, humbly, in the next thing and the next.

In our times with God we should also, I believe, confess our faith. I once heard someone urge Christians, 'Give yourselves believing time,' and I think this is right. We need not only to ask for grace but also to exercise faith by saying what we believe

39

—not necessarily the creeds which we may say in church, but our own individual creeds.

We might say something like: 'I believe that you are my perfect righteousness and my mighty inner life. I believe that the Holy Spirit lives in me and that, with your help, I have the strength for all the things that are your will for me. I believe that for every temptation I have a way of escape. In the light of these beliefs, I have yielded myself to you and ask you to help me with the results of that surrender. So I go into this day, this hour, to live by faith in you; and I believe this day will be a day of peace, of love, of truth, of loyalty to you, of power by your Spirit to do and bear for you. On you I rest and in your name I go, Lord Jesus Christ.'

H. C. G. Moule

I know that there are certain mental and emotional and moral and spiritual attitudes that are anti-health: anger, resentments, fear, worry, desire to dominate, self-preoccupation, guilts, sexual impurity, jealousy, a lack of creative activity, inferiorities, a lack of love. So in prayer I've learned to surrender these things to Jesus Christ as soon as they appear.

E. Stanley Jones

Arguing with God

I would . . . fill my mouth with arguments.   **Job 23:4**

God wants us to plead with him and bring our strong reasons because this will show that we feel the value of his mercy. When a person searches for arguments for a thing, it is because he attaches importance to it. Also, our use of argument teaches us the ground on which we obtain the blessing. The person pleading is made to understand intensely that it is by grace alone that a sinner obtains anything from the Lord.

Here are a few of the arguments that have been used with great success with God.

God's attributes: Abraham laid hold of one of these when he pleaded for Sodom: 'Will not the Judge of all the earth do right' (Genesis 18:25)? So we can take hold of the justice, the mercy, the faithfulness, the wisdom, the long-suffering, the tenderness of God.

God's promises: Solomon, at the opening of the temple, pleads with God to remember the word which he had spoken to his father David and to bless that place (1 Kings 8:25ff). If we have a divine promise, we may plead with certainty.

The great name of God: Moses pleaded God's honour and asked, 'Why should the Egyptians say, "It was with evil intent that he brought them out, to kill them in the mountains and to wipe them off the face of the earth"?' (Exodus 32:12); and Joshua asked God, 'What . . . will you do for your own great name' (Joshua 7:9)? We too can plead with God for his great name's sake.

The sorrows of God's people: Jeremiah calls on the Lord to look at his suffering people (Lamentations 4:6ff) and before long his cries are heard. When we see God's people brought very low, we can use that as our plea for God to return and save us.

The past: David pleaded this: 'You have been my helper. Do not reject or forsake me, O God my Saviour' (Psalm 27:9). We are dealing with an unchanging God who will do in the future what he has done in the past because he never turns from his purpose.

The sufferings, death, merit and intercession of Jesus Christ: I am afraid we do not understand what it is that we have at our command when we are allowed to plead with God for Christ's sake. This is virtually what Christ says to us, 'If you need anything of God, all that the Father has belongs to me; go and use my name.' When you plead the name of Christ, you plead something which shakes the gates of hell and which the hosts of heaven obey, and God himself feels the sacred power of that divine plea.

C. H. Spurgeon

Ordering Our Cause Before God

I would state my case before him.   **Job 23:4**

As a petitioner comes into court with his case well prepared, so we should approach the King of kings with premeditation and preparation, knowing what we are doing, where we are and what we want. We should feel that we are doing something that is real; that we are about to address ourselves to God, whom we cannot see but who is really present; whom we can neither touch nor hear but who is as truly with us as though we were speaking to a flesh-and-blood friend.

It is not well to beat round the bush in prayer but to come directly to the point. Ask for what you need now. I like the prayer of Abraham: 'If only Ishmael might live under your blessing' (Genesis 17:18). There is the name and the person prayed for and the blessing wanted—all put in a few words. Let our words be few and our hearts fervent.

We should also take a look at the blessing we want, to see whether it is a fitting thing to have asked for. A little reflection would show some of us that some things which we want were better let alone. And mingled with the acceptable prayer, there must be the salt of submission to will of God.

C. H. Spurgeon

2

The Range of Prayer
(All human life is here)
Part II

Meditation: Thinking in God's Presence

May my meditation be pleasing to him, as I rejoice in the Lord. **Psalm 104:34**

Studying the Bible tells us about God. But meditation 'looks' at God's truth in a way that stimulates a response, getting us deeper into God's word, and his word deeper into us. There are two main ways:

Imaginative meditation: Taking a passage or verse, explore the pictures and sensations it suggests. For instance, with Psalm 36:9b, 'In your light we see light,' you might imagine the sun rising, or a lamp being lit in a dark room. As you enter into your mental picture, you may become aware of how light gradually or suddenly exposes what is hidden, shows up the true situation, helps us find the way . . . This expands our view of God's truth.

Contemplative meditation: Use a few words to still your mind and focus it on God. For instance, try repeating Psalm 36: 9b silently. After a while you might just say 'light' or perhaps, 'Make me see.' Rather than expanding our ideas, this kind of prayer expands our sense of God's presence, holiness and love.

There are many variations on these basic patterns. You can use your imagination on a gospel story, picturing its sights, sounds, smells, the emotions of those involved and looking on; or explore a biblical theme like 'desert' or 'living water'.

You can hold a word or phrase in your mind, repeating it when your thoughts wander; or focus on a mental image like kneeling at Jesus' feet or being held in God's arms like a child.

Always start with relaxation. Sit comfortably upright with back supported, both feet on the floor, hands loose in your lap. Breathe in deeply and let all the breath out again. Then breathe gently and steadily.

Remember meditation is to help you to come close to a God who is already nearer to you than you can imagine. Don't be tied to methods; experiment to find what suits you.

Veronica Zundel[37]

Christian meditation goes far beyond the notion of detachment. There is need for detachment but we must go on to attachment: detachment from the confusion all around us in order to have a richer attachment to God and to other human beings.

Richard Foster[38]

After having placed yourself in the presence of God by an act of loving faith, you must read something that is substantial and stop gently upon it; not that you may reason, but only to fix your mind. A firm belief of God being present in the ground of our hearts must needs engage us to sink down into ourselves, gathering all the thoughts inwards and hindering them from being scattered abroad.

Madame Guyon

Meditation is the activity of calling to mind, and thinking over, and dwelling on, and applying to oneself, the various things that one knows about the works and ways and purposes and promises of God. It is an activity of holy thought, consciously performed in the presence of God, under the eye of God, by the help of God, as a means of communion with God. Its purpose is to clear one's mental and spiritual vision of God, and to let his truth make its full and proper impact on one's mind and heart. It is a matter of talking to oneself about God and oneself, reasoning oneself out of moods of doubt and unbelief into a clear apprehension of God's power and grace. Its effect is ever to humble us, as we contemplate God's greatness and glory and our own littleness and sinfulness, and to encourage and reassure us as we contemplate the unsearchable riches of divine mercy displayed in the Lord Jesus Christ.

J. I. Packer[39]

Like the hub of a wheel, the meditation on Scripture becomes the central reference point by which all other meditations are kept in proper perspective. Take a single event like the resurrection or a

47

parable or a few verses or even a single word and allow it to take root in you. Seek to live the experience. Smell the sea. Hear the lap of the water along the shore. See the crowd. Feel the sun on your head and hunger in your stomach. Taste the salt in the air. Touch the hem of his garment.

Richard Foster[40]

The name of Jesus is both light and nourishment. Are you not strengthened in the spirit when you meditate on it? As honey to the taste, as melody to the ear, as songs of gladness in the heart, so is the name of Jesus. And medicine it is as well. Nothing but the name of Jesus can restrain the impulse of anger, repress the swelling of pride, cure the wound of envy and put to flight impure and ignoble thoughts. For when I name the name of Jesus, I call to mind a man conspicuous for every honourable and saintly quality and also, in the same person, the almighty God—so that he both restores me to health by his example and makes me strong by his assistance.

Bernard of Clairvaux

Enjoying God

Though the fig tree does not bud . . . yet I will rejoice in the Lord, I will be joyful in God my Saviour.

Habakkuk 3:17, 18

We . . . rejoice in God through our Lord Jesus Christ, through whom we have now received reconciliation.

Romans 5:11

The joy of the Lord is your strength.   **Nehemiah 8:10**

You will fill me with joy in your presence, with eternal pleasures at your right hand.   Psalm 16:11

Send forth your light and your truth, let them guide me; let them bring me to your holy mountain, to the place where you dwell. Then will I go to the altar of God, to God, my joy and delight.   Psalm 43:3, 4

I will . . . take delight in my people.   Isaiah 65:19

O God, you are my God, earnestly I seek you; my soul thirsts for you, my body longs for you, in a dry and weary land where there is no water.   Psalm 63:1

The longing of the soul for God only makes itself felt when all lesser delights and earthly joys are relegated to their right place. If you are not conscious of this soul-thirst, it is because your heart is trying to satisfy itself from the world and is engaged in digging wells that can hold no water. Jesus said, 'Blessed are those who hunger and thirst for righteousness, for they will be filled' (Matthew 5:6).

Can we say of God, 'You are *my* God'? He is ours but we must seek him. We must, as it were, build the fences of our faith in an ever-enlarging enclosure of God. It is not enough for the emigrant to have a claim. He must open up the resources that lie buried in his piece of land. The diamonds of the Cape were first discovered by a child playing with a white stone but they have been sought ever since.

The fact is that our longings after God are the response of our hearts to the beat of his heart and to the knock of his hand. Prayer is the response of our nature to the circulation of his life-blood in us.

F. B. Meyer

49

Perhaps this is the day you can begin to spend less time in asking and more time in rejoicing in God. Not for what he can give us, not that we may be used, that the glory of our name or of our organisation may be magnified; not that we might have power with God and men for ourselves. But to forget ourselves and to pray for one purpose and to one end only—the joy and satisfaction and glory of our Saviour. May he teach us always to remember that our goal is God himself, not joy, nor peace, nor even blessing, but himself, our God.

Kenneth N. Taylor[41]

God is the joy of the hearts of those who love him. To love God is to find the secret of joy which is deep and abiding because it is inward and spiritual. Ordinary human happiness as the word denotes (it comes from 'hap', to chance or happen), depends on outward events, on the changing and capricious circumstances of life. Christian joy, the joy of the Christian believer, is independent of circumstances and finds its source in the unchanging God.

Frank Colquhoun[42]

Sometimes I consider myself as a stone before a carver, whereof he is to make a statue: presenting myself thus before God, I desire him to make his perfect image in my soul, and render me entirely like himself.

At other times when I apply myself to prayer, I feel all my spirit and all my soul lifted up without any care or effort of mine, and it continues as it were suspended and firmly fixed in God, as in its centre and place of rest.

The soul which thus enjoys God desires nothing

but him.

Brother Lawrence

When communion becomes real, prayer becomes delight. Love seeks the company of its object, simply for the sake of being in the presence of the beloved one. Do we not love God enough to shut ourselves in with him at times just to enjoy him?

A. T. Pierson

When we turn our eyes to the sun and keep them wide open in that direction, they are filled with the glory of the light; so, when we raise our minds and hearts towards God and, so far as in us lies, keep open all the avenues of communication with him, his light, his joy and his strength fill the whole being, and through his work, thus unhindered in us, he enables us to grow in wisdom and understanding, and to increase in the knowledge and love and joy and peace of God.

Shirley C. Hughson[43]

There are many ways of coming to the stillness of prayer and no single method is the absolute and only path. It is God's work, anyway, so we could not possibly dictate how he is to work in any of us. All we are doing is learning to open ourselves up to him, setting the scene; then we hand over to God . . .

A short word or phrase . . . can lead us into peaceful communion with God when we repeat it during a quiet time. Gradually we realise that as well as loving God, we are being loved by him. It is like sun-bathing: we face the light and absorb it in a still act of surrender. We have to stop thinking about what we are doing and just get on and do it. The heart of contemplative prayer is standing completely exposed and empty before God. As we gently let go of our rattling thoughts, we move into the sort of loving which does not need words. We find ourselves in tune with the silence at the heart of all creation . . .

There are times in ordinary life when words are totally inadequate. When someone faces intense grief there is nothing you can say, because their emotion goes beyond our everyday concepts and thoughts. Great happiness can also reduce us to silence. I remember being speechless with joy when each of my babies was first put into my arms.

It is a sign of good friendship if you can be to-gether without carrying on a non-stop conversation. We are all familiar with the opposite situation, when you are introduced to someone at a party and struggle to keep the conversation going with a mutual lack of interest. Close friends going for a walk or spending a day together do not have to talk all the time; they can simply enjoy being with each other. It is a moving experience to be with an elderly couple who have been happily married for years. Their quiet contentment as they sit together says more than an anthology of love poetry.

The same applies to our relationship with God. The Pharisees poured out many words to him, thinking that there was some virtue in their verbal clutter. Of course we often do need to use words in prayer. But our friendship with God will not deepen much if we can never stop talking when we are with him. When we manage to be still and open and ready to listen, we give God space to work in us in ways we never imagined.

Angela Ashwin[44]

Silent Listening Before God

Be still, and know that I am God.   **Psalm 46:10**

Be still before the Lord, all mankind, because he has roused himself from his holy dwelling. **Zechariah 2:13**

Be still before the Lord and wait patiently for him.
                            Psalm 37:7

There is . . . a time to be silent and a time to speak.
                     Ecclesiastes 3:1, 7

The Lord is in his holy temple; let all the earth be silent before him.   **Habakkuk 2:20**

Listen and hear my voice; pay attention and hear what I say.   **Isaiah 28:23**

It is not necessary to maintain a conversation when we are in the presence of God. We can come into his presence and rest our weary souls in quiet contemplation of him. Our groanings, which cannot be uttered, rise to him and tell him better than words how dependent we are upon him.

O. Hallesby[45]

Whenever the sounds of the world die out in the soul, then we hear the whisperings of God. He is always whispering to us, only we don't always hear because of the noise, hurry and distractions which life causes as it rushes on.

F. W. Faber

People who have any maturity in the spiritual life know that there is a listening side to prayer. Not all prayer is made up of our human speaking. It is both courteous and highly profitable not only to talk to God but also to listen to him.

W. E. Sangster[46]

If our life is poured out in useless words, we will never hear anything in the depths of our hearts, where Christ lives and speaks in silence.

Thomas Merton

Silence is the doorway through which we pass to a deeper understanding of Christ's prayer for the world, and the deeper listening in which it results marks the transition from the more active forms of prayer, such as meditation, to a quieter and more receptive contemplative prayer.

Mother Mary Clare[47]

Contemplative prayer was to be a rich source of listening to God. Day by day I would sit or stand or kneel in my prayer room, relax, allow tensions to slide away, focus on God, and a miracle would happen. As I closed my eyes to shut out visual stimuli, and as I closed my ears, as it were, by dealing authoritatively with the distractions which threatened my ability to tune in to God, it was as though, on the one hand, I closed a series of shutters on the surface level of my mind, thus holding at bay hindrances to hearing the still, small voice of God, and on the other hand, I released a trigger which gave deeper, inner, hidden parts of myself permission to spark to life. As I attempted to focus, deliberately and unashamedly on the presence of Christ, I would sometimes detect an inner stirring as though secret antennae were being roused and alerted to pick up any and every signal the indwelling royal guest might choose to give.

Joyce Huggett[48]

Practising the Presence of God

In him we live and move and have our being.
Acts 17:28

Where can I go from your Spirit? Where can I flee from your presence? If I go up to the heavens, you are there; if I make my bed in the depths, you are there. If I rise on the wings of the dawn, if I settle on the far side of the sea, even there your hand will guide me, your right hand will hold me fast.   **Psalm 139:7–10**

Nothing in all creation is hidden from God's sight. Everything is uncovered and laid bare before the eyes of him to whom we must give account.   **Hebrews 4:13**

Remain in me, and I will remain in you . . . I am the vine; you are the branches.   **John 15:4, 5**

Whether you eat or drink or whatever you do, do it all for the glory of God.   **1 Corinthians 10:31**

Everything God created is good, and nothing is to be rejected if it is received with thanksgiving, because it is consecrated by the word of God and prayer.
1 Timothy 4:5

Although we need to set aside some time each day for specific prayer, it's good to practise the presence of God wherever we go: walking along the street, driving a car, riding a bicycle, sitting at home or in the office, working at a bench. Anywhere and everywhere we can turn our thoughts to God, thanking him for anything good that has happened, asking for his help for what we're about to do, confessing our anger or selfishness, praying for someone in need; in other words, sharing our lives with him and talking to him as we would talk to our best and closest friend.

David Watson[49]

Through every grass blade in the thousand, thousand grasses; through the million leaves, veined and edge-cut, on bush and tree; through the songnotes and the marked feathers of the birds; through the insects' hum and the colour of the butterflies; through the soft warm air, the fleck of clouds dissolving—I used them all for prayer.

Richard Jefferies

Practise the presence of God! Hold fellowship with him! Even in business, or in the midst of daily toil, often lift your heart for a moment into the atmosphere of his presence. Our business is the absolute surrender of our heart to him.

On waking—turn your mind at once to him. If you wake slowly, let each step to wakefulness be a step towards him. Address to him your first words of the day. Say in your heart, 'I am here, Lord, and eager for another day.'

Cultivate the custom of linking your Lord and yourself with 'we'. 'What are we going to do together today, Lord?' If it seems too familiar at first, remember that he encourages such intimacy. It is beyond our understanding why he should want to live in our soiled hearts, but he does. Say 'we'.

Glance ahead at the day. 'We are going to do everything together today, Lord.' See yourself going through the day with him. Meet every known duty in thought with him before you meet it (still with him) in reality. 'We must make the most of that opportunity, Lord.' 'We must be particularly watchful there, Lord.'

Then rise with zest and begin your day.

W. E. Sangster

The real problem of the Christian life comes where people do not usually look for it. It comes the very moment you wake up each morning. All your wishes and hopes for the day rush at you like wild animals. And the first job each morning consists simply in shoving them all back; in listening to that other voice, taking that other point of view, letting that other larger, stronger, quieter life come flowing in. And so on, all day. Standing back from all your natural fussings and frettings, coming in out of the wind.

We can only do it for moments at first. But from those moments, the new sort of life will be spreading through our system: because now we are letting him work at the right part of us. It is the difference between paint which is merely laid on the surface and a dye or stain which soaks right through.

C. S. Lewis[50]

Jesus knew how to look at life. He was able to find God in earth and sky and sea, in city and temple, in the home and in the desert. But he also found him in the hungry, the thirsty, the naked, the imprisoned. Today he would expect us, if we have learnt how to look at life as God sees it, to find him in the urban priority areas, the streets of Calcutta, the relief camps of Ethiopia and the rubbish dumps of Latin America with their scavenging population.

In fact, if we know how to look at life, we shall . . . find God in all things. He spoke not simply of the beauties of nature or of man-made creations, but of experiences and circumstances, of the wider sphere of contemporary affairs, of relationships, work, leisure, disappointments, brokenness—some of which might, on the surface of things, seem more calculated to reveal evil than God, but the seeing eye will find God in the unexpected. Jesus himself certainly found God in the 'common things of life, its goings out and in . . . in each duty and each deed, however small and mean'. Heavenly wisdom was rooted in earthly reality. Prayer did not lead him into the realm of philosophical thought, ideas and abstract concepts, but into the material. It was the lost coin of a woman's head-piece, lamps under bushels, children piping and dancing in the village square, badly patched garments, or burst wine skins, that became the substance of his reflection. The domestic details, far from being divorced from prayer, reinforced for him spiritual truths.

Sister Margaret Magdalen[51]

When God is always present to our mind, when we are constantly making use of him, when we find ourselves naturally turning to him through the hours of the day, then such quiet peace and rest settle down upon us that we cannot be moved by any anxiety of the present or future.

F. B. Meyer

There is not in the world a kind of life more sweet and delightful than that of a continual conversation with God: those only can comprehend it who practise and experience it. Yet I do not advise you to do it from that motive; it is not pleasure which we ought to seek in this exercise; but let us do it from a principle of love and because God would have us.

I began to live as if there was none but he and I in the world. I worshipped him the oftenest I could, keeping my mind in his holy presence, and recalling it as often as I found it wandering from him. Every hour, every minute, even in the height of my business, I drove away from my mind everything that was capable of interrupting my thought of God.

When we are faithful to keep ourselves in his holy presence, and set him always before us, this not only hinders our offending him and doing anything that may displease him, at least wilfully, but it also begets in us a holy freedom and, if I may so speak, a familiarity with God wherewith we ask, and that successfully, the graces we stand in need of. By often repeating these acts they become *habitual,* and the presence of God is rendered as it were *natural* to us.

Brother Lawrence

To get the most vivid sense of God's presence, all thought of people and this world must be shut out and all interruptions avoided that come through the senses or the imagination. Only as we learn the art of thinking only on God will we learn the great lessons of secret prayer.

Haste in such prayer prevents that calmness, concentration, peace and rest which are so necessary. He who rushes into the presence of God, to hurry through a few formal petitions and then back to outside cares and pursuits, does not stay long enough to fix his mind's gaze on the unseen and eternal. The spirit, disturbed and perturbed, tossed up and down and driven to and fro by worldly thoughts and cares, can no more become a mirror to reflect God, than can a ruffled lake become the mirror of the starry sky arching above it.

A sense of the presence of God, trained in secret prayer, has power to reveal sin. Secret prayer is always a revelation of self as well as of God. But all such self-revelation brings blessing, for it is the result of a vision of God; and God's answer to such self-abasement is a new communication and exaltation. Daniel abhors himself, but hears a voice saying, 'Do not be afraid, Daniel. Since the first day that you set your mind to gain understanding and to humble yourself before your God, your words were heard, and I have come in response to them' (Daniel 10:12). Isaiah bewailed his unclean lips, but the seraph touched those same lips with a live coal from God's altar and said, 'See, this has touched your lips; your guilt is taken away and your sin atoned for' (Isaiah 6:7). Even Peter, who felt so unfit for the companionship of the Lord that he involuntarily begged Christ to go away from him, heard only the reassuring answer, 'Don't be afraid; from now on you will catch men' (Luke 5:10).

A sense of the presence of God has the power, also, to prevent sin. When Joseph was in the crisis of temptation, his answer to his tempter was an obvious sign of his habit of thinking of God. He had evidently learnt that great truth: 'You are the God who sees me' (Genesis 16:13). He practised the presence of God and it was natural for him to ask, 'How . . . could I do such a wicked thing and sin against God?' (Genesis 39:9) Paul reminds the Corinthian Christians that they are the very temple of God and, on the basis of this fact, exhorts them: 'Let us purify ourselves from everything that contaminates body and spirit, perfecting holiness out of reverence for God' (2 Corinthians 7:1). It is easy and natural to do what pleases God when we feel that he is with us—creating, upholding and strengthening.

A sense of the presence of God can give us courage in witnessing for him. Elijah's characteristic phrase was, 'As the Lord, the God of Israel, lives, whom I serve . . .' (1 Kings 17:1), as though he felt himself to be constantly in the presence of his Master, watching and waiting to be beckoned or guided by a glance. It was because he was before God as one who waits for and receives orders and messages, that he could stand unabashed before Ahab and Jezebel.

The practice of the presence of God is the secret of faithfulness and cheerfulness in doing our ordinary duties. Paul wrote, 'Each one should remain in the situation which he was in when God called him' (1 Corinthians 7:20). When the renewing grace of God finds a person engaged in an honest calling, however humble, he has no need to change his vocation but only to take a new and divine partner into his daily work. Brother Lawrence cultivated the habit of thinking of God as being with him all the time, until his convent kitchen became like the Garden of Eden and every day like a day of heaven on earth.

This sense of the divine presence prompts the highest outbursts of thanksgiving as we get glimpses of God's character and glory. It also prompts worship—which ascribes worth to God and keeps before ourselves and others his infinite excellence. Such worship includes thanksgiving and praise but rises above both in adoration, in which our whole spirit goes out to God in words or, more likely, in wordless groanings and raptures— the language of emotions and affections.

A. T. Pierson

We are always present with him who sees all and keeps all things in existence by the very act that knows their existence. But we are more present to him when we are aware of his nearness to us than when we ignore it. For then the presence is conscious and mutual: it is the presence of a person to a person. And it is only when we are thus present to him that we truly discover ourselves as we really are.

Thomas Merton

The instruction to pray *always* does not mean we are to neglect the ordinary duties of life; what it means is that the soul which has come into intimate contact with God in the silence of the prayer-room is never out of conscious touch with the Father; that the heart is always going out to him in loving communion; and that the moment the mind is released from the task upon which it is engaged it returns as naturally to God as the bird does to its nest. What a beautiful conception of prayer we get if we regard it in this light, if we view it as fellowship, an unbroken audience with the King. Prayer then loses every vestige of dread which it may once have possessed; we regard it no longer as a duty which must be performed, but rather as a privilege which is to be enjoyed, a rare delight that is always revealing some new beauty.

F. B. Meyer

Engaging in Conflict

Our struggle is not against flesh and blood, but against the rulers, against the authorities, against the powers of this dark world and against the spiritual forces of evil in the heavenly realms. Therefore put on the full armour of God ... and pray in the Spirit on all occasions with all kinds of prayer and requests.

Ephesians 6:11, 12, 13, 18

Your enemy the devil prowls around like a roaring lion looking for someone to devour. Resist him, standing firm in the faith. **1 Peter 5:8, 9**

Being in anguish, [Jesus] prayed more earnestly, and his sweat was like drops of blood falling to the ground. When he rose from prayer and went back to the disciples, he found them asleep, exhausted from sorrow. 'Why are you sleeping?' he asked them. 'Get up and pray so that you will not fall into temptation.'

Luke 22:44–46

When you fast, put oil on your head and wash your face, so that it will not be obvious to man that you are fasting, but only to your Father, who is unseen; and your Father, who sees what is done in secret, will

reward you. **Matthew 6:17, 18**

Natural instinct—and spiritual struggle

Raising palm trees in Greenland would be an unnatural proceeding. They were never intended to grow there, and never can grow there save under stress of artificial forcing. The culture of prayer would be just as strained a procedure, were it not that the tendency to pray is native to us, that prayer is indigenous in us, that we *do* pray, one way or another, even though fitfully and without effect, and that men always have prayed and always will pray. The definition of man as a praying animal, while not comprehensive, is certainly correct.

H. E. Fosdick[52]

Praying, though from one standpoint the most natural thing a Christian ever does, since crying to his heavenly Father is a Spirit-wrought instinct in him, is always a battle against distractions, discouragements and deadenings from Satan and from our own sinfulness. Prayer is not easy, and although spontaneity is of its essence we have to make a dogged discipline of it or else it would get crowded out—Satan would see to that!

Only through the energising Holy Spirit, who gives the awareness and the desire from which prayer springs, the thoughts and words in which it is voiced and the persistence in it which God commands, does prayer ever become all that it is meant to be.

J. I. Packer[53]

Spiritual war

That prayer is one aspect of spiritual warfare is clearly taught in Scripture (Ephesians 6:11, 12, 18, 19). In this aspect of prayer, three and not two are involved. Between God and the devil—the god of this world—stands the praying man. Though pitifully weak in himself, he occupies a strategic role in this truceless warfare. His power and authority as he battles in faith are not inherent, but are his through union with the Victor of Calvary.

In a graphic illustration our Lord likened Satan to a well-armed strong man who kept his palace in peace. Before he could be dislodged and his captives liberated, Jesus said, he must first be bound. Only then could the rescue be effected (Matthew 12:28, 29; Luke 11:21, 22).

What does it mean to bind the strong man if not to restrain his activity by appealing to the conquering power of him who was manifested to destroy— render inoperative, powerless—the works of the devil (1 John 3:8)? And how can this be done but by the prayer of faith which lays hold of the victory of Calvary and believes for its manifestation in the situation on which prayer is being focused?

J. Oswald Sanders[54]

Not many Christians have been trained in Satan-defeating intercession. Few exercise the divine power which is available to demolish strongholds (2 Corinthians 10:3, 4). Still fewer know how to resist the devil so that they see him flee before them (James 4:7). Ephesians 6:10–18 is the passage we must examine to learn about this type of intercession. How many Christians live equipped and clothed with the full armour of God, to stand firm in the day of evil? We will not be effective intercessors until we have learnt to overcome Satan.

I believe the key to Ephesians 6:10–17 is to be found in verse 18. Prayer is not another piece of armour, or else the analogy has broken down. Neither is prayer a development of the sword of the Spirit. Prayer enables us to use the armour. It is our contact point with the army of evil. Prayer is the battlefield.

Tim Pain[55]

Spiritual wrestling

The idea of wrestling is associated with prayer. It is not suggested that we wrestle with God, but there is a grip and grappling that calls for vigilance and concentration. It is quite clear that prayer is not the easy thing that seems to be implied in the simplicity of asking our heavenly Father for what we want and getting it. There is travail in it. There is work in it. There is entreaty in it. There is importunity in it. Maybe Coleridge was not far wrong when he spoke of prayer as the highest energy of which the human heart is capable and the greatest achievement of the Christian's warfare on earth.

Samuel Chadwick

Fasting

Fasting according to the New Testament pattern would seem to be the spontaneous outcome of:

the challenge of a special test or temptation;
a deep yearning for a closer walk with God;
a heavy burden for the spread of the gospel in
the regions beyond;
spiritual travail for the upbuilding of the

church;
        the exigencies of a stubborn situation.
One obvious value of fasting lies in the fact that its
discipline helps us to keep the body in its place. It is
a practical acknowledgment of the supremacy of
the spiritual. But in addition to this reflex value,
fasting has direct benefits in relation to prayer as
well. Many who practise it from right motives and
in order to give themselves more unreservedly to
prayer testify that the mind becomes unusually
clear and vigorous. There are a noticeable spiritual
quickening and increased power of concentration
on the things of the spirit.

J. Oswald Sanders[56]

Darkness, dryness, desolation

My God, my God, why have you forsaken me?
                                        Matthew 27:46

**The Lord is close to the brokenhearted and saves those
who are crushed in spirit.   Psalm 34:18**

When someone is at his wits' end, it is not a cowardly
thing to pray; it is the only way he can get in touch
with reality. 'O that I might get in touch with the
reality that explains things!'

Oswald Chambers

. . . in the desert you stay put unless you are firmly,
even visibly, moved on. Scuttering about—whether
physically or spiritually—like so many terrified rats
in a burning house, will only lead to disaster . . . It
is always a temptation to run out of the desert at
the wrong level, as it were; to kill its pain, to substi-

tute the real winter by a spring we make for ourselves ... However much we resent the desert, however much we rail against its hellish quality, the settled conviction of the authors of Exodus and of all mystical writings since is that God is there in the desert with us. It is not that he pushes us out to endure the emptiness, the loneliness, the meaninglessness, while he gets on with something more important; much less that he gets some kind of satisfaction from watching us writhe in pain or simply die on our feet—or on our knees. No, the conviction of the authors of the Exodus is that he is there, with them, sharing their wanderings, their experience of strangeness and their alienation.

Charles Elliott[57]

In desolation remember two things: know that the desolation will pass; if you can keep the focus of your attention on God, even if you have no felt experience of his presence, he will teach you through the desolation. He is, as it were, gouging out your false securities, revealing himself to your own inner emptiness so that he may fill and possess it.

If we imagine ourselves to be in the hands of God as clay is in the hands of the potter, then we can see desolation as a turning of the clay so that it becomes a vessel which can contain life-giving water which as unformed clay it could not hold.

Gerard W. Hughes[58]

I should like to say this to people who are suffering from darkness or dryness in their prayer—or from both: try not to fuss. Don't blame yourself. Don't force yourself spiritually. Try, if you possibly can, to keep the time you have set yourself to pray, even if all that you can do in that time is to say words or to read a book. Above all, try to trust—even though it will be a blind trust. Trust and wait. Wait for something to happen. God may be testing your love, deepening your prayer, changing your way of prayer, changing your whole God-focus. Wait and see in blind trust . . .

If you can manage to persevere in silent prayer, you will discover, slowly but surely, a sense of deep peace underneath all the stress, a deep security underneath all the insecurity and almost a deep sense of joy underneath all the gloom.

Evan Pilkington[59]

3

Effective Prayer
(Getting it right)
Part I

Right Relationship (You and God)

O God, you are my God, earnestly I seek you; my soul
thirsts for you, my body longs for you, in a dry and
weary land where there is no water ... On my bed I
remember you; I think of you through the watches of
the night ... I stay close to you; your right hand up-
holds me.   Psalm 63:1, 6, 8

You perceive my thoughts from afar ... Before a word
is on my tongue you know it completely, O Lord.
                                            Psalm 139:2, 4

Personal and private
When you pray, go into your room, close the door and
pray to your Father, who is unseen. Then your Father,
who sees what is done in secret, will reward you.
                                            Matthew 6:6

Very early in the morning, while it was still dark, Jesus got up, left the house and went off to a solitary place, where he prayed ... He travelled throughout Galilee preaching in their synagogues and driving out demons.   Mark 1:35, 39

As he was praying, heaven was opened and the Holy Spirit descended on him in bodily form like a dove. And a voice came from heaven: 'You are my Son, whom I love; with you I am well pleased.'
                                                      Luke 3:21, 22

Jesus went out into the hills to pray, and spent the night praying to God. When morning came, he called his disciples to him and chose twelve of them.
                                                      Luke 6:12, 13

When Jesus was praying in private and his disciples were with him, he asked them, 'Who do the crowds say I am?'   Luke 9:18

[Jesus] said to [his disciples], 'Pray that you will not fall into temptation.' He withdrew about a stone's throw beyond them, knelt and prayed, 'Father, if you are willing, take this cup from me; yet not my will, but yours be done.' ... Being in anguish, he prayed more earnestly, and his sweat was like drops of blood falling to the ground.   Luke 22:40–44

After he had dismissed [the crowd], he went up into the hills by himself to pray.   Matthew 14:23

Crowds of people came to hear him and to be healed of their sicknesses. But Jesus often withdrew to lonely places and prayed.   Luke 5:15, 16

Jesus chose *the early morning hours* for prayer. Many of the mightiest men of God have followed his example in this. That absolute concentration on God which is essential to the most effective prayer is most easily possible in the early morning hours. The first thing we should do each day is to be alone with God and face the duties, the temptations and the service of that day and gain strength from God for all of it.

Sometimes Jesus spent *the entire night* in prayer. If we set apart a whole night for prayer, there will be no hurry; there will be time for our hearts to become quiet before God and for our minds to be brought under the guidance of the Holy Spirit; time to pray things through. A night of prayer should be put entirely under God's control. We should lay down no rules as to how long we will pray or as to what we shall pray about, but be ready to wait on God for a short time or a long time and to be led in one direction or another as he wills.

Jesus prayed *before all the great crises of his earthly life.* He prayed before choosing the twelve disciples; before the sermon on the mount; before starting out on an evangelistic tour; before being anointed with the Holy Spirit and starting his public work; before announcing to the twelve his approaching death; before the cross. He prepared for every important crisis by a lengthy time of prayer. Whenever any crises of life is seen to be approaching, we, too, should prepare for it by a time of very definite, unhurried prayer to God.

Jesus prayed not only before but also *after his great achievements and important crises.* When he had fed the five thousand with five loaves and two fishes and the crowd wanted to make him king, he sent them away and went up into the mountain apart to pray. So he went from victory to victory. It is more common for most of us to pray before the great events of life than after them, but if we would pray *after* the great achievements, we might go on to still greater ones; as it is, we are often puffed up or exhausted, so we go no further.

Jesus gave special time to prayer *when life was unusually busy.* Apparently the busier his life was, the more he prayed. Many have learnt this secret from Christ; others have lost their power because, instead, they allowed increasing work to crowd prayer out.

Jesus prayed *before the great temptations of his life.* The victory of Calvary was won in the Garden of Gethsemane. Many temptations come on us unawares and all we can do is cry to God for help, then and there; but others we can see approaching and, in such cases, the victory should be won before the temptation really reaches us.

For Jesus prayer was exacting, all-absorbing, paramount. It was the call of a sweet duty to him, the satisfying of a restless yearning, the preparation for heavy responsibilities and the meeting of a vigorous need. Jesus was, above all else, a man of prayer. And he spent his strength and time in teaching people how to speak to God, to commune with him, to be with him.

Jesus lived and suffered under the law of prayer. He could do nothing without prayer and all things by prayer. The apostles, also, were helpless without prayer—and were absolutely dependent on it for success in defeating their spiritual enemies. They could do all things by prayer.

E. M. Bounds

A private place and time

Every praying person needs some place and time for prayer, free from needless interruption and intrusion. Our Lord counsels us, when we pray, to get somehow, somewhere, a silent, secret, communing place with God as the very basis of prayer and of all the holy living which is built on prayer. There are secrets of soul and spirit which no other human being, however intimate, ought to know or, indeed, can know; but from God we can conceal nothing. God's eye pierces to our secret rooms; he reads the thoughts and hears the words that are as yet unspoken.

Why is such stress laid on this closing in of the praying person with God? Isn't it, first of all, in order to practise the presence of God? Nothing else has so marvellous an effect on character and conduct as this sense of God's presence. Such a sense of God's presence may be cultivated. God has appointed two means to this end: first, a meditative reading of Scripture and secondly, habitual communion with God in our secret, private place.

To concentrate all thought and desire on God, to forget all else in order not to forget him, and so to be lost in the absorbing sense of his presence—this is the first secret of power in prayer and, in fact, the secret also of all power in holy living and serving.

The secret place is also the great school for the education of the spiritual sense. Imagination is the sense of the unseen; reason, the sense of truth and falsehood; conscience, the sense of right and wrong; sensibility, the sense of the attractive and repulsive; memory, the sense of the past. The understanding and heart have eyes with which to see God's beckoning and glance; ears with which to hear his still, small voice, organs of touch with which to handle him and see that it is he himself.

Let us think of the secret room as a place of vision—of contemplation of God, which makes possible new impressions, new discoveries into his nature, new revelations of his goodness, new gifts of his power. So, before we call, he answers and while we are yet speaking, he hears. Communion proves to be mutual—an outgoing and an incoming, a voice that answers as well as a voice that cries.

A. T. Pierson

Secret prayer is a necessity. Why? Because such prayer gives special opportunities for cultivating a deep, individual insight into yourself and your personal needs, and into the Lord Jesus Christ, into God in Christ, in all his glory and grace *for you.* You cannot minimise your solitary, secret, individual times of confession, petition, praise and thanks without the results that are to be expected. Your spiritual life will be feebler. Your whole renewed nature and its work will suffer from the centre.

H. C. G. Moule

The desert became a safe place in which Elijah could dispel the weariness of a drained condition. There he heard the still small voice of God as David might have heard it in the night hours in his sleeping room. The shoreline where Jesus cooked an early morning breakfast for the tired disciples became a safe place for the defeated Simon Peter who must have wondered whether he would ever get a second chance.

Where are your safe places and mine? . . . Where is it that God can meet us and share his secrets?

I speak of the secrets of his power and glory, the affirmations of his steadfast love, the promises of his willingness to help when we are at wits' end, the offer of parent-like protection, the extension of his strong hand of stability and guidance . . .

I have established a safe place in my home where I pursue an encounter with God each morning. For me it is my study; for others it could be a bedroom, a kitchen or a corner in the basement. It must be a place away from other people and varying interferences as much as possible.

Other versions of the safe place can be realised. Some of us will find them where we work or at other localities within the circumference of our daily journeys.

Occasionally we need to enter the safe places set aside by the Christian community for us all to use.

Gordon Macdonald[60]

A private name for God

Unless we can find the right name for God, we have no free, real, joyful, open access to him. As long as we have to call God by general terms like, 'The Almighty', 'The Lord God', as long as we have got to put 'the' before the word to make it anonymous, to make it a generic term, we cannot use it as a personal name. But there are moments when the sacred writers, for instance, burst out with something which has the quality of a nickname. Remember the psalm in which, after more restrained forms of expression, suddenly David bursts out, 'You, my Joy!' That is the moment when the whole psalm comes to life. Saying, 'O you our Lord', 'O you are the Almighty', and the like was stating to God facts about him, but bursting out and saying,

'O you my Joy!' was quite a different thing. And when we can say to God, 'O you my Joy!' or when we can say, 'O you the pain of my life, O you who are standing in the midst of it as torment, as a problem, as a stumbling block!' then we have established a relationship of prayer. I am quite certain that if some day, 'O you my Joy!' or any other cry of this kind bursts out of you, it will be the moment when you will have discovered a relationship between him and you which is your own.

In human relationships there are surnames, there are Christian names, there are nicknames. It is good if you can have a nickname by which you can call the Almighty God, a nickname that has all the depth of your heart, all the warmth you are capable of; it becomes your way of saying, 'In my uniqueness this is the way I perceive your uniqueness.' Come out with the words which are your own and call God by the name which he has won in your own life. At that moment you will have met. In the ever deepening and enriching relationship that follows you will have a great deal of time to discover other words, to discard the words of hatred and anguish. Like the martyrs spoken of in the book of Revelation you will say, 'Just and true are your ways' (Revelation 15:3). And these words then will wipe out all the words of bitterness, all the names that sound cruel; but you will keep the names which are personal, which are your own, and which will be a real relationship and a real way of being related to the living God.

Archbishop Anthony Bloom[61]

Two-way
This is what the Lord says, he who made the earth, the

Lord who formed it and established it—the Lord is his name: 'Call to me and I will answer you and tell you great and unsearchable things you do not know.'

Jeremiah 33:2, 3

Prayer should be a two-way communication. Since there is no voice of God speaking in the room, you need to learn how he speaks in the silence of your heart and mind. I believe this takes practice and experience. Ask God to help you to know his will. If a thought keeps returning to you, talk it over with others. Don't act hastily. Not every thought that pops into your head while you are praying is from God.

Kenneth N. Taylor[62]

Prayer is not meant to be a monologue but a dialogue. It is a communion, a friendly talk. While the Lord communicates with me mainly through his word, he gives me a great deal of comfort in a direct manner. By 'comfort' I do not mean cuddling or coddling but assurance—assurance of his presence and his pleasure in my service. It is like the comfort given by a military commander to his soldier or envoy whom he sends on a difficult mission: 'You go, put on your armour, I'm watching you, and I'll send you all the reinforcements you need as they are needed.' I don't just assume that God is near me and pleased with me; I must have a fresh witness daily.

S. L. Brengle

True prayer is the whole nature going out to God in adoration, thanksgiving, confession, supplication, intercession and also being fully open to receive incoming blessing.

A. T. Pierson

Prayer, in its essence, is fellowship with God; it is talking and listening to and loving the Supreme Being who made and maintains this universe.

W. E. Sangster[63]

Weak sinner—strong Saviour

Two men went up to the temple to pray, one a Pharisee and the other a tax collector. The Pharisee stood up and prayed about himself, 'God, I thank you that I am not like other men—robbers, evildoers, adulterers—or even like this tax collector. I fast twice a week and give a tenth of all I get.' But the tax collector stood at a distance. He would not even look up to heaven, but beat his breast and said, 'God, have mercy on me, a sinner.' **Luke 18:9–13**

You say, 'I am rich; I have acquired wealth and do not need a thing.' But you do not realise that you are wretched, pitiful, poor, blind and naked. I counsel you to buy from me gold refined in the fire, so that you can become rich; and white clothes to wear, so that you can cover your shameful nakedness; and salve to put on your eyes, so that you can see. **Revelation 3:17, 18**

We come to God in prayer, first of all, for forgiveness. There are crookednesses in our life which we must straighten out and roughnesses which we must make smooth, and these things can only be done by coming in penitence to God's mercy-seat, while, like the tax collector, we cry out, 'God, have mercy on me, a sinner.'

But, in order to receive mercy, we need to exercise mercy. No one can truly appeal for forgiveness while cherishing an unforgiving and vindictive spirit towards others.

In the parable of the two debtors (Matthew 18: 23–35), Jesus shows us the impossibility of receiving if we do not give forgiveness. Even the formal declaration of forgiveness which followed the confession of debt and bankruptcy, was cancelled and revoked when the person who had been forgiven the immense debt of ten thousand talents, took by the throat his fellow-servant who owed him one hundred pence, and mercilessly cast him into prison despite his entreaties. The greater debtor had been utterly bankrupt and yet had found compassion and release; but he would not exercise similar compassion towards one whose debt was so small that payment would follow patience. In him there was neither the grace of pity nor of patience; and he who after forgiveness was too hard-hearted to forgive, showed himself incapable of really receiving or even recognising forgiveness.

A. T. Pierson

What we must start with if we wish to pray is the certainty that we are sinners in need of salvation, that we are cut off from God and that we cannot live without him and that all we can offer God is our desperate longing to be made such that God will receive us, receive us in repentance, receive us with mercy and with love.

Archbishop Anthony Bloom[64]

There are things in us which are a hindrance to our prayers. These hindrances are what the Spirit of prayer points out to us.

First and foremost there is our selfishness. We

live and move in such a narrow circle that the Spirit of prayer cannot create in our hearts true zeal for others. However the Spirit can convict us of this sin. And as soon as I acknowledge my selfish indifference, he will save me from it.

Secondly there is our love of ease. That is why Jesus admonishes us to watch and pray. The apostle [Paul] speaks of it as striving in prayer. To strive in prayer means to be so watchful at all times that we can notice when we become slothful in prayer and go to the Spirit of prayer to have this remedied.

O. Hallesby [65]

The devil and his minions have no interest in seeking to detach our minds from a study of Greek or mathematics; but he is tremendously interested in distracting us in every possible way the moment he sees us trying to pray.

There is much of distraction in the power of sinners like ourselves for which the tempter is not responsible. In many instances it is our own fault. Every sin we commit, every distraction we wilfully allow, makes it more difficult the next time to concentrate in prayer, and we . . . pile up trouble for ourselves in the future. We create a distracted habit of mind, and the mind works . . . as it has been trained. We cannot, therefore, attribute everything to the agency of the tempter.

Shirley C. Hughson [66]

Many people want to pray well but find themselves stangely hindered. The two chief hindrances are enslavement to feeling and wandering thoughts.

The Bible in its realism does not present us with

an idyllic picture of an élite stripped of all natural weakness; it shows us people like you and me who carry the whole weight of their inborn temperaments. There are strong people like Elijah, hotly pursuing the priests of Baal. There are weak people like Jeremiah, beset by the temptation to remain silent. There are people full of contradictions like Jacob, David or Peter who alternated between sublime impulses and treachery.

And if we suffer the continuing slavery of our natures, the Bible shows us that we do not necessarily have to be freed from it in order to experience the power of God. God takes hold of these people just as they are. He comforts Elijah when the prophet is in despair at the failure of his miracles. He strengthens Jeremiah and draws him out of his silence.

Only Jesus Christ, God incarnate, is seen to be at once completely human and completely exempt from strong or weak reactions. He is always free because he is always loved by the Spirit. Nevertheless he shares our weaknesses and our strengths: our weariness, disappointments and despair; our enthusiasm, joys and ardour. He remained silent before Pilate but took a whip in the court of the Temple. He had compassion on the weak but violently attacked the strong. He cried out in anguish on the cross but proclaimed his divinity with authority. And yet his words and actions never have the automatic character of psychological reactions. He is neither strong nor weak in the human and natural meaning of these words.

He is alive. If we open our hearts to him, he fills them with his presence. In so far as he thus lives in us we are delivered from our weak reactions while at the same time becoming more aware than ever of our weakness. We are delivered also from our strong reactions, while at the same time receiving from him a strength that is beyond compare.

For he alone answers the deep-rooted anguish which we hide under our apparent reactions. Through him we can both accept our weakness and overcome it. Then from within society we can help to break the tragic vicious circles which throw it into disorder and drive it into war, suffering and oppression. And we can point it to the true remedy for its ills: faith in Jesus Christ.

Paul Tournier[67]

Unique individual and loving Lord
I am God Almighty. **Genesis 17:1**

The Lord is the everlasting God, the Creator of the ends of the earth. **Isaiah 40:28**

I am the Lord, the God of all mankind. **Jeremiah 32:26**

Even the very hairs of your head are all numbered.
Matthew 10:30

He determines the numbers of the stars and calls them each by name. **Psalm 147:4**

God has arranged the parts of the body, every one of them, just as he wanted them to be. **1 Corinthians 12:18**

We have different gifts, according to the grace given us. **Romans 12:6**

As we approach the holy God, we should take time to remember that he is:

All-powerful, giving to all without having to take
    anything away from anyone or from himself;
All-knowing, seeing our most secret intentions;
Truthful, never failing to keep any of his promises;
Faithful, never forsaking anyone who trusts in him;
Loving, with a love which even our countless sins
    cannot exhaust;
Majestic, setting his glory above the heavens;
Long-suffering, remaining strong and patient
    though provoked every day;
Just, not clearing the guilty, but
Merciful, forgiving sin;
Compassionate, waiting to be gracious;
Good, with a goodness which leads to repentance;
Pure, hating sin, but inviting the sinner to turn to
    him.

H. More, T. Cadell

In prayer, we approach God, the judge of all.
When Moses stood before God on the mountain,
he trembled with fear. But we may come with bold-
ness, although God is a consuming fire, because in
Christ Jesus we stand accepted.

F. B. Meyer

Prayer is essentially . . . a love affair with God, not
schemes or techniques or ways of prayer, but the
most direct, open approach of each one of us as a
person to God our creator, redeemer and sanctifier.
This is something beyond all methods and ideas.
We are seeking God himself, not thoughts about
him, nor about ourselves in relation to him.

    Prayer is an adventure at the end of which we
stand face to face before the living God; not in a
vague way in a place which we call heaven, but in

the here and now of our lives.

Mother Mary Clare[68]

In this vast universe how can we picture God as caring for every individual thing, even to stricken sparrows and to the hairs of our head? Consider, however, the scientific truth of gravitation, that the whole earth rises to meet a child's ball, just as truly as the ball falls to meet the earth; and that only the lack of sensitiveness in our instruments prevents us from measuring the earth's ascent as it responds to the pull of the child's toy. Can we imagine that? Is it not unimaginable, though plainly true? And if in a gravitate system a whole planet moves to meet a tossed ball, we ought not to dismiss, for reasons of weak imagination, the truth that in a love-system of persons, the eternal God responds to each child's approach.

Prayer involves confidence that God takes an interest in the individual who prays. The fact, for example, that the Bible is pre-eminently a book of prayer, involves of necessity the companion fact that the God of the Bible cares for individuals. He knows all the stars by name (Psalm 147:4); he numbers the hairs of our heads (Matthew 10:30); of all the sparrows 'not one of them is forgotten by God' (Luke 12:6). John is expressing his thought of God as well as his interpretation of Christ when he says, 'He calls his own sheep by name' (John 10:3).

God is like a shepherd who misses even one lost sheep from his flock, a housewife who seeks for a single coin, a father who grieves for one boy gone wrong (Luke 15). Of all the children in the world, says Jesus, 'Your Father in heaven is not willing that any of these little ones should be lost'

(Matthew 18:14).

H. E. Fosdick.[69]

Prayer is, among other things, being all by yourself with God; face to face—a human being and his maker; the lover and the beloved; the child and his father.

Gonville ffrench-Beytagh[70]

Every man must be allowed to pray in his own way. It is far from being true that the most valuable temperament in religion is the mystical. God needs us all. Some are . . . stolid, patient, undemonstrative; some are . . . high-spirited, nervous, passionate; some are hopeful, cheerful, light-hearted; some are sombre and serious. There are as many temperaments as there are people, and each has his own problems and his peculiar way of expressing the spirit of Christ. The first step in useful living for many folk is the recognition of God's purpose in making us on such unique and individual plans. He evidently likes us better that way . . .

Nothing could be more intensely individual than the prayers of the Bible. Nobody tries to commune with God in anyone else's way.

H. E. Fosdick[71]

Friend with friend

You are my friends if you do what I command . . . I have called you friends, for everything that I learned from my Father I have made known to you.

John 15:14, 15

Abraham . . . was called God's friend.   **James 2:23**

Keep yourselves in God's love.   **Jude 21**

THE PRAYER ADVENTURE

Prayer is a cumulative life of friendship with God.
H. E. Fosdick[72]

How much our friends mean to us! Remember each act and bond of love; think of all that we may trust them for and all the times they have stood by us. Then think of God as being all that and infinitely more; our friend: the one who is personally interested in us; who has come near us in the intimacy of fellowship; who has promised us so much and done so much for us; who has made priceless sacrifices for us and is ready to take any trouble, go to any expense, to help us.

He is a friend in need. He has told us to claim his help specially at such times. 'Call upon me in the day of trouble; I will deliver you' (Psalm 50: 15). 'God is our refuge and strength, an ever present help in trouble' (Psalm 46:1). 'God, who comforts the downcast', 'the Father of compassion and God of all comfort' (2 Corinthians 7:6; 1:3), are his chosen titles. So we needn't be afraid when we have nothing to bring to him but our grief and fear. We shall be welcome. He is seated on his throne for the very purpose of giving us help in time of need, however hopeless and dark things seem.

He is a friend for all seasons. In one of Jesus' parables (Luke 11:5–10), a man went to his friend asking for something when all reasonable grounds for expecting a favour was out of the question. It was midnight and the door was shut. Even so, the door was opened, the petition heard and the favour granted. Whatever we are to understand by the reluctant earthly friend in the story, our heavenly Friend will not be prevented by any cause from hearing and helping us in the most extreme and desperate situations.

A. B. Simpson

The same growth ought to take place in our relationship with God which occurs between a parent and his child. At first the child wants the parents' gifts and thinks of the parents largely in terms of the things which they do for his comfort and pleasure. He is not able yet to appreciate the value of the parents' personalities. A sure sign of wholesome maturity is found in the child's deepening understanding of the parents themselves—his increasing delight in their friendship, thankfulness for their care, acceptance of their ideals, reliance on their counsel and joy in their approval. The child grows through wanting things from his parents into love of his parents for their own sakes.

H. E. Fosdick[73]

If you are [God's] friend, he will share his thoughts and plans with you. If you are his partner, he will be concerned about your views on his plans and projects. Whatever else prayer may be, it is intended to be a sharing and a taking counsel with God on matters of importance to him. God has called you to attend a celestial board meeting to deliberate with him on matters of destiny.

You can see how this raises the whole level of prayer. It is not intended primarily to be centred in my petty needs and woes. To be sure, God is interested in them. They have a place on his agenda. But the agenda itself has been drawn up in heaven and deals with matters of greatest consequence.

John White [74]

At its deepest level, prayer is fellowship with God: enjoying his company, waiting on his will, thanking him for his mercies, committing our lives to him, talking to him about other people as well as ourselves, and listening in the silence for what he has to say.

Billy Graham[75]

Child and parent
Which of you, if his son asks for bread, will give him a stone? Or if he asks for a fish, will give him a snake? If you, then, though you are evil, know how to give good gifts to your children, how much more will your Father in heaven give good gifts to those who ask him!
Matthew 7:9–11

Which of you fathers, if your son asks for a fish, will give him a snake instead? Or if he asks for an egg, will give him a scorpion? If you, then, though you are evil, know how to give good gifts to your children, how much more will your father in heaven give the Holy Spirit to those who ask him!
Luke 11:11–13

As a father has compassion on his children, so the Lord has compassion on those who fear him.
Psalm 103:13

My son, do not despise the Lord's discipline and do not resent his rebuke, because the Lord disciplines those he loves, as a father the son he delights in.
Proverbs 3:11, 12

The Father himself loves you because you have loved me and have believed that I came from God.
John 16:27

You did not receive a spirit that makes you a slave

again to fear, but you received the Spirit of sonship. And by him we cry, '*Abba,* Father.' The Spirit himself testifies with our spirit that we are God's children . . . heirs of God and co-heirs with Christ. **Romans 8:15–17**

Because you are sons, God sent the Spirit of his son into our hearts, the Spirit who calls out, '*Abba*, Father.'
Galatians 4:6

How great is the love the Father has lavished on us, that we should be called children of God!   **1 John 3:1**

Through [Jesus] we . . . have access to the Father by one Spirit. Consequently, you are . . . members of God's household.   **Ephesians 2:18, 19**

Prayer moves God not as an orator moves his hearers but as a child moves his father. Two words of a child, humbled and crying, will prevail more than carefully prepared speeches.

John Bunyan

I have never forgotten the dread that gripped me when, as a youth, I was invited to go for an interview at the manse. I walked past the door several times before I had the courage to ring the bell, and as I stood at the door my heart throbbed in my ears. Imagine my surprise when shown into the room, to find the great man on all fours, giving a ride to riotously happy children, who had turned his long beard into driving reins. He was their father! They knew nothing of the awe in which others stood of him, and as they grew older and knew something of his greatness, their reverence deepened but their fearlessness was not diminished.

The children of the house are free and fearless.

Samuel Chadwick

I have a twenty-year-old son, and I cannot imagine him walking into our house and saying to me, 'Oh, thou chairman of the sociology department at Eastern College, Oh thou who doth clothe me, feed me and provide me with every good and perfect gift; I beseech thee this day, lend me the car.' That's not the way he talks to me. I'm his daddy. So, like a good Italian boy, he walks into the house, throws his arms around me, kisses me and says, 'Hi Dad, can I borrow the car?' You see, we love each other.

Jesus wants each of us to be intimate with him. That is why the apostle Paul tells us that we should not pray as people filled with fear, but we should talk to God as one who is closer than any father could ever be. Actually, the apostle Paul instructs us to address God as *'Abba,'* which is the ancient Hebrew word for 'daddy'.

Tony Campolo[76]

Jesus teaches two things about the fatherhood of God which are to be our constant encouragement and inspiration in prayer. First, that he knows how to give good gifts to his children and, second, that he wills to give even the Holy Spirit to those who ask him. The child of God who has the sense of sonship comes boldly to one who is both able and willing.

In illustrating God's fatherhood in Matthew 7: 9–11 and Luke 11:11–13, Jesus contrasts three things: the bread, which is the staff of life, with the stone, which the Jews thought of as dead and used to kill people who blasphemed or were disobedient; the fish, a form of animal food, with the serpent, the symbol of the devil, who destroys instead of nourishing; the egg, which contains the germ of reproduction, with the scorpion, whose sting is painful and often fatal.

The broad lesson is that our Father in heaven both knows how to give good gifts to those who ask him and is more willing than earthly parents to give us all that we ask or need; and how to withhold when that would be the wiser course and the better way of giving. For we don't know what we should pray for. We make the mistake of asking for the stone when we think it to be bread; or for what would prove to be a venomous curse or a stinging disappointment if we were to have it. And so we trust our Father to keep back what would only feed our selfish lusts or damage us, and to give us instead what will make for true spiritual life.

A. T. Pierson

Prayer is the intelligent communication between a child and his heavenly Father. The first view of God given in the Lord's Prayer is not of God's majesty but of his fatherly love. This must have sounded strange to the listening disciples. Never had they or any other Jew heard God so named, at least in relation to the individual. He was sometimes called the Father of the Nation but no sinful person had every dared to call God his Father. They had probably heard Jesus speak of God as *his* Father but it had probably not dawned on them that *they* should call Jehovah by such a name. Yet Jesus really meant that we may and should recognise that God is our Father in the very sense in which he is his Father and ours as sharing his sonship and name. The name expresses the most personal tender love, protection, care and intimacy; and it gives to prayer the beautiful atmosphere of home.

God is our father. Much more than you love your child does he love you; much more than you would give or sacrifice, he is ready to give and has already sacrificed; much more than you can trust or ask a father for, you may dare to bring to him; much more unerring is his wisdom, unlimited his power and inexhaustible his love.

A. B. Simpson

Jesus tells us to respond to God by saying 'Father'. We may say it in an agonised cry of desperation or with affection and love and thanksgiving, but it is the most basic of man's words before God, and if we can say it and mean it, then the whole of life takes on a different perspective. Love and joy, or pain and loneliness, whatever grief or separation you may have, it all happens within the fatherhood of God. 'Underneath are the everlasting arms.' Whatever my sin or desperation, if I can say, 'Abba, Father,' I proclaim that I am a son of God—not a slave or a servant but a son. (That is what the story of the prodigal son is about.) But I remain a son of God because I belong with Jesus, the Son of God. With him I say, '*Abba*, Father'.

Gonville ffrench-Beytagh[77]

Prayer for Jesus was also '*Abba*' at the level of an adult conversation between Father and Son—an intimate conversation of shared secrets, a responsible one of shared purpose. His whole identity was wrapped up in this conversation . . . His life had meaning only in so far as he was a response to his Father's will, a reflection of his Father's glory, an utterance of his Father's word, a baptism into the Father's heart of love, an all-consuming passion for union with the Father breathed out in a response of lovelonging and desire.

Sister Margaret Magdalen[78]

Right Living (The Pray-er's Life)

The prayer of a righteous man is powerful and effective.   James 5:16

No good tree bears bad fruit, nor does a bad tree bear good fruit. Each tree is recognised by its own fruit. People do not pick figs from thorn-bushes, or grapes from briars. The good man brings good things out of the good stored up in his heart, and the evil man brings evil things out of the evil stored up in his heart. For out of the overflow of his heart his mouth speaks.
Luke 6:43–45

Offer your bodies as living sacrifices, holy and pleasing to God—which is your spiritual worship. Do not conform any longer to the pattern of this world, but be transformed by the renewing of your mind. Then you will be able to test and approve what God's will is—his good, pleasing and perfect will.   Romans 12:1, 2

Everyone who confesses the name of the Lord must turn away from wickedness.   2 Timothy 2:19

Not everyone who says to me, 'Lord, Lord,' will enter the kingdom of heaven, but only he who does the will of my Father who is in heaven.'   Matthew 7:21

Prayer is not a mere episode of the Christian life. Rather the whole of life is a preparation for and the result of prayer.

Prayer is sensitive and always affected by the character and conduct of him who prays. Prayer is dwarfed, withered and petrified when faith in God is staggered by doubts of his ability, or through the shrinking caused by fear. When faith has a telescopic far-off vision of God, prayer works no miracles and brings no marvels of deliverance. But when God is seen by faith's closest and fullest eye, prayer makes a history of wonders.

E. M. Bounds

We should try to believe as we pray, think as we pray, feel as we pray and act as we pray. Prayer must not be a solitary, independent exercise but inseparably connected with our lives and what we do. Prayer is an incentive to useful living but not a substitute for it.

The person whose heart has been set in motion by prayer, and whose spiritual pulse quickened by Scripture, has work to do.

He has a responsibility to feed the poor, comfort the sad, help the distressed, teach the ignorant and soothe the depressed. At home, he has his family to teach, watch over and be an example to.

But his most difficult work will be on himself. He has to watch against all sorts of sins, errors and temptations which he will find heavier in weight and more in number the more closely he looks at them: against prejudice; against impatience when his wisely thought out plans are defeated; against cold and heartless prayer; against over-anxiety about things. He has to watch because he finds that he does not show, as clearly as he might, in his life, the attitude that he has when on his knees before God; that his best obedience is incomplete; that his faith, though sincere, often lacks energy; that it is difficult to 'take captive every thought to make it obedient to Christ' (2 Corinthians 10:5).

He may have to watch against the fear of man, as he may find it easier to endure the cross than to despise the shame; or against an eager desire for popularity; to watch in order to keep himself unspotted from the world—to hold the things of the world with a loose hand—and to achieve consistency of character.

He will want to walk with God—not merely bow down before him at stated intervals, or address him ceremoniously on great occasions and then retreat and live at a distance, but walk with him—communicate intimately, naturally and continually with him.

H. More, T. Cadell

People would pray better if they lived better. They would receive more from God if they lived lives that were more obedient and pleasing to God. We would have more strength for intercession if we did not have to spend so much of it, as it were, settling up old scores and paying overdue taxes. Our time alone with God is often spent in taking out a decree of bankruptcy—it could have a notice above it saying, 'Closed for repairs'—instead of being a time of great spiritual wealth for ourselves and others.

Those whose lives are true and obedient, who—over and above that—are doing things to make God glad, can come eagerly to meet their Father, not simply to be forgiven but to be approved of and to receive.

We pray feebly because we live feebly. The stream of praying cannot rise higher than the fountain of living. We cannot talk strongly to God when we have not lived strongly for him. The prayer time cannot be made holy to God when the life has not been made holy to God. Scripture emphasises that our conduct gives value to our praying: 'Then you will call, and the Lord will answer; you will cry for help and he will say: Here am I. If you do away with the yoke of oppression, with the pointing finger and malicious talk, and if you spend yourselves on behalf of the hungry and satisfy the needs of the oppressed . . .' (Isaiah 58:9, 10).

E. M. Bounds

Our prayer will be fruitless unless we are grafted and rooted in the Vine, daily drawing up the precious, life-giving sap of the Holy Spirit.

Audrey Merwood[79]

Right Priorities (First Things First)

God's will, God's kingdom, God's glory

Seek first his kingdom and his righteousness.
Matthew 6:33

Hallowed be your name, your kingdom come, your will be done on earth as it is in heaven . . . for yours is the kingdom and the power and the glory forever.
Matthew 6:9–13

This is the assurance that we have in approaching God:

that if we ask anything according to his will, he hears us. And if we know that he hears us—whatever we ask —we know that we have what we asked of him.

1 John 5:14, 15

If you remain in me and my words remain in you, ask whatever you wish, and it will be given you.   John 15:7

Ask the Lord of the harvest ... to send out workers into his harvest field.   Luke 10:2

Pray for us that the message of the Lord may spread rapidly and be honoured.   2 Thessalonians 3:1

Always keep on praying for all the saints.

Ephesians 6:18

The Lord's Prayer, the pattern prayer, teaches us that we must take the whole world into our praying, and that we must see clearly that the line of its redemption is that of return to comformity to the will of God, made possible by the life, death and resurrection of the one who taught us this prayer.

G. Campbell Morgan[80]

Jesus seems to have given the Lord's Prayer (Matthew 6:9–13; Luke 11:2–4) as a model of real prayer, Christian prayer, in distinction to the prayers of the Pharisees and heathen (Matthew 6: 5–8).

The error of the hypocrite is selfishness. Even in his prayers he is obsessed with his own self-image and how he looks in the eye of the beholder. But in the Lord's Prayer Christians are obsessed with God—with his name, his kingdom and his will, not with theirs. It is therefore the exact opposite of the exhibitionism of hypocrites who use prayer as a vehicle for their own glory.

The error of the heathen is mindlessness. He just goes babbling on, giving voice to his meaningless liturgy. He does not think about what he is saying, for his concern is with volume not content. But God is not impressed by verbiage. Over against this folly, Jesus invites us to make all our needs known to our heavenly Father with humble thoughtfulness, and so express our daily dependence on him.

Thus Christian prayer is seen in contrast to its non-Christian alternatives. It is God-centred (concerned for God's glory) in contrast to the self-centredness of the Pharisees (preoccupied with their own glory). And it is intelligent (expressive of thoughtful dependence) in contrast to the mechanical incantations of the heathen.

John R. W. Stott[81]

In compassion for the miseries of mankind, we rightly pour out our hearts in prayer for the poor and destitute, but we should not forget to pray, also, for those who are blinded by too full an enjoyment of the good things of this life. When Paul prayed for his friends, he did not ask for an increase of their wealth, power, fame, or for any other form of outward prosperity. He prayed instead that they might be strengthened by God's power through his Spirit in their inner being; that Christ might dwell in their hearts through faith; that they might be rooted and established in love; that they might have the power to grasp the vast dimensions of Christ's love; that they might be filled with all the fullness of God (Ephesians 3:14–19). These are the sort of petitions which we need never hesitate to present; the requests which we can be sure are in line with God's will; the intercessions which will be of benefit when wealth, fame, power will be forgotten things.

Why did Paul pray night and day that he might see his Thessalonian converts again? Not merely to have the pleasure of seeing people he loved; but that he might supply what was lacking in their faith (1 Thessalonians 3:10). Here was a man who had so much of heaven in his friendships that his deepest prayers for them were not for worldly blessings.

H. More, T. Cadell

We must accept gladly the fact that, much as our heavenly Father encourages us to bring everything to him in prayer, and much as he loves to answer and bless, we are to seek first his kingdom—and make his purposes primary in our lives.

If we really pray from the heart in terms of John 15:7, then we are openly saying to the Lord, 'You choose in what way I can glorify you.' It may be his will to glorify himself through strengthening us to triumph in and over a lifetime's affliction. Think of the testimonies you have heard and Christian lives you have seen. Some have been snatched from disaster and others have shone in the midst of pain.

Michael Baughen[82]

God has his will in heaven; we are to discover that will; then we are to ask that it be done; after that we are to believe we have received it; finally we are by faith to proclaim it into being.

Ken Gardiner[83]

The first thing in prayer is to find God's purpose; the second, to make that purpose our prayer. Prayer is finding out God's purpose for our lives and for the earth and insisting that that shall be done.

S. D. Gordon

Many people shrink from God's will. They think it always means pain or sorrow or bereavement. They always feel melancholy when you speak of doing the will of God. How the devil has libelled God! The will of God is the will of a father. It is the fatherhood of God going out in action.

In our own life, we shall never be really right or happy until we have got to the point of saying, 'I delight to do your will, O God.' We may not *begin* there. The first step is to choose it; then we shall come to accept it lovingly and thankfully; but, finally, we shall rejoice and delight in it. If you cannot say, 'You will be done,' say, 'I am willing to be made willing that your will should be done.'

F. B. Meyer

There is no prayer so mighty, so sure, so full of blessing as, 'Your will be done.' It is not the death-knell of all our happiness, but the pledge of all possible blessing.

God's children do not really believe that it is possible to know God's will. Or, if they believe this, they do not take the time and trouble to find it out. What we need is to see clearly in what way it is that the Father leads his waiting, teachable child to know that his petition is according to his will. It is through God's word, taken up and kept in the heart, the life, the will; and through God's Holy

Spirit, accepted in his indwelling and leading, that we shall learn to know that our petitions are according to his will.

Andrew Murray

How shall we know that will? At the very least, we may always know it by his word and promise. We may be very sure that if we ask anything that is covered by a promise of his word, we may immediately turn that promise into an order on the very bank of heaven.

A. B. Simpson

Can we know the will of God? Can we know that any specific prayer is according to his will? We most surely can. How?

First, by the word of God. God has revealed his will in Scripture. When anything is definitely promised in the word of God, we know that it is his will to give that thing.

For example, when I pray for wisdom, I know that it is the will of God to give me wisdom, for it says so in James 1:5 ('If any of you lacks wisdom, he should ask God, who gives generously to all without finding fault; and it will be given to him'). So when I ask for wisdom, I know that the prayer is heard, and that wisdom will be given me. In the same way, when I pray for the Holy Spirit, I know from Luke 11:13 ('If you then, though you are evil, know how to give good gifts to your children, how much more will your Father in heaven give the Holy Spirit to those who ask him') that it is God's will, that my prayer is heard, and that I have the petition I have asked of him.

Here is one of the greatest secrets of prevailing

prayer: to study Scripture to find what God's will is, as revealed there in the promises, and then simply take these promises and spread them out before God in prayer with the absolutely unwavering expectation that he will do what he has promised in his word.

But there is another way in which we may know the will of God, and that is by the Holy Spirit. There are many things that we need from God which are not covered by any specific promise. But we are not left in ignorance of God's will even then. In Romans 8:26, 28 we are told: 'We do not know what we ought to pray, but the Spirit himself intercedes for us with groans that words cannot express. And he who searches our hearts knows the mind of the Spirit, because the Spirit intercedes for the saints in accordance with God's will.' Here we are distinctly told that the Spirit of God prays in us, draws out our prayer, in the line of God's will. When we are thus led by the Holy Spirit in any direction, to pray for any given object, we do it in all confidence that it is God's will, and that we are to receive the very thing we ask.

The passage 1 John 5:14, 15 is one of the most abused passages in the Bible. The Holy Spirit put it into the Bible to encourage our faith. Often, when we wax confident in prayer, someone will say, 'Don't be too confident. If it is God's will, he will do it. You should put in, "If it be your will".' Doubtless there are many times when we do not know the will of God, and in all prayer submission to the excellent will of God should underlie it; but when we know God's will, there are no 'if's; and this passage was not put into the Bible in order that we might introduce 'if's' into all our prayers, but in order that we might throw 'if's' to the wind, and have *confidence* and *assurance,* and *know* that we have the petitions which we asked of him.

R. A. Torrey

Prayer for others should be the basic burden of our prayer life. For Christians love is the law of life. We have been captured by the love that God showed us in Christ when he entered our human plight and brought meaning to it. This love is to be shared, not hoarded. Prayer for others is one of the best ways of loving.

If prayer for others is one way to show our love then our prayer for others ought to deal with the deepest, most pressing needs that others have. What kind of things do I pray about? How do I move beyond selfishness in prayer? How do I focus on really important requests so that I pray more and more according to God's will?

One suggestion is to follow the example of the apostle Paul (see 1 Thessalonians 3:11–13). This is intercession at its best. The deep basic needs of his friends are brought before God. The highest, brightest purposes of God in their lives are sought: an increase of love and holiness.

Pray that those you know may have spiritual insight. The aim of this insight is to know the will of God: his programme and purposes for his people. The result of this insight is to live a life pleasing to God.

I should also pray that lives intertwined with mine shall be given power to cope with the problems that life throws at them. The purpose of this power is our endurance with joy and thanksgiving.

Physical and financial needs are important; we

should not forget them. But we should also make sure that our priorities in prayer follow the priorities of God. What higher favour can we do for others than to lift their names before God asking him to catch them up in his plan and to give them a share in carrying it out?

David A. Hubbard[84]

Pray for all saints—God's holy ones—throughout the church, that the Spirit of holiness may rule them. Pray that the power of the Holy Spirit may so work the love of God in believers that the world may see and know God's love in them. Pray for the power of the Spirit in the church. Pray that every convert may know that he can claim and receive the fullness of the Spirit.

Andrew Murray

In Jesus' name

I will do whatever you ask in my name, so that the Son may bring glory to the Father. You may ask for anything in my name, and I will do it . . . On that day you will realise that I am in my Father, and you are in me, and I am in you.   **John 14:13, 14, 20**

If you remain in me and my words remain in you, ask whatever you wish, and it will be given you . . . The Father will give you whatever you ask in my name.

John 15:7, 16

In that day you will no longer ask me anything. I tell you the truth, my Father will give you whatever you ask in my name. Until now you have not asked for anything in my name. Ask and you will receive, and your joy will be complete . . . In that day you will ask in my name. I am not saying that I will ask the Father on

your behalf. No, the Father himself loves you because you have loved me and have believed that I came from God.   **John 16: 23, 24, 26, 27**

Another angel, who had a golden censer, came and stood at the altar. He was given much incense to offer, with the prayers of all the saints, on the golden altar before the throne. The smoke of the incense, together with the prayers of the saints, went up before God from the angel's hand.   **Revelation 8:3, 4**

If I go to a bank and hand in a cheque with my name signed to it, I ask of that bank in *my own name*. If I have the money deposited in the bank, the cheque will be cashed; if not, it will not be. If, however, I go to a bank with somebody else's name to the cheque, I am asking in *his name*, and it does not matter whether I have money in that or any other bank; all that matters is whether the person whose name is signed to the cheque has money there. If he does, the cheque will be cashed.

So it is when I go to the bank of heaven – when I go to God in prayer: I have nothing deposited there, I have absolutely no credit there in my own name; so if I go in my own name, I will get absolutely nothing. But Jesus Christ has unlimited credit in heaven, and he has granted me the privilege of going to the bank with his name on my cheques; and when I go in his name, my prayers will be honoured to any extent.

To pray, then, in the name of Christ is to pray on the ground, not of my credit, but his; to renounce the thought that I have any claims on God whatever and to approach him on the ground of Christ's claims. Praying in the name of Christ is not merely adding the phrase, 'I ask these things in

Jesus' name', to my prayer. I may put that phrase in my prayer and really be resting on my own merit all the time. On the other hand, I may omit that phrase but really be resting on the merit of Christ all the time. But when I really approach God not on the ground of my merit but on the ground of Christ's merit, not on the ground of my goodness but on the ground of the atoning blood, God will hear me.

R. A. Torrey

It is Christ, the Son, who has the right to ask what he will; it is through our abiding in him and his abiding in us that his Spirit breathes in us what he wants to ask and obtain through us. We pray in his name: the prayers are really ours and as really his.

To pray in the name of Jesus is to pray in unity, in sympathy, with him. As the Son began his prayer by making clear his relation to his Father, pleading his work and obedience and his desire to see the Father glorified, do so too. Draw near and appear before the Father in Christ. Plead his finished work. Say that you are one with it, that you trust in it, live in it. Say that you too have given yourself to finish the work the Father has given you to do, and to live alone for his glory. And ask then confidently that the Son may be glorified in you. This is praying in the name, in the very words, in the Spirit of Jesus, in union with Jesus himself. Such prayer has power. If with Jesus you glorify the Father, the Father will glorify Jesus by doing what you ask in his name.

Andrew Murray

To pray in Christ's name means something more than adding 'for Christ's sake' to our petitions. The name expresses personality, character and being. The person is the name. Prayer in Christ's name is prayer according to the quality of his person, according to the character of his mind and according to the purpose of his will. To pray in the name of Christ is to pray as one who is at one with Christ, whose desires are the desires of Christ and whose purpose is one with that of Christ.

In the prayer in the name, all conditions are unified and simplified in him. Motive is judged in the name. Prayer is proved in the name. Prayer is sanctified in the name. Prayer is endorsed by the name, when it is in harmony with the character, mind, desire and purpose of the name.

To pray in Christ's name means more than that. We are heard for his sake. He is the petitioner. When I was in Leeds, a man came along to look over some works in which he was interested. He wrote to the firm and his request was politely declined. No argument could get him beyond the little shutter in the outer office. He told his disappointment to a friend, who suggested I might be able to help. He came to see me. I gave him my card and wrote to the head of the firm. Next day, he presented his request and handed in my card. Immediately every door was opened to him. His petition was granted but not for his own sake. The head of the firm saw me in him. In a similar way, we pray in Christ's name. He endorses our petitions and makes our prayers his own, and the Father hears him pray.

Samuel Chadwick

The relationship of prayer is through Jesus. And the prayer itself must be offered in his name because the whole strength of the case lies in Jesus. As we come in Jesus' name, it is the same as though Jesus prayed. It is the same as though Jesus put his arm in yours and took you up to the Father and said, 'Father, here is a friend of mine; we're on good terms. Please give him anythng he asks, for my sake.' And the Father would quickly bend over and graciously say, 'What will you have? You may have anything you ask when my Son asks for it.' That is the practical effect of asking in Jesus' name.

But in the ultimate analysis, the force of using Jesus' name is that he is the victor over the traitor prince. Prayer is repeating the victor's name into the ears of Satan and insisting on his retreat. As one prays persistently in Jesus' name, the evil one must go. Reluctantly, angrily, he must loosen his clutches and go back.

S. D. Gordon

Through the Holy Spirit
We do not know what we ought to pray, but the Spirit himself intercedes for us with groans that words cannot express. And he who searches our hearts knows the mind of the Spirit, because the Spirit intercedes for the saints in accordance with God's will.   Romans 8:26, 27

Through him [Jesus] we . . . have access to the Father by one Spirit.   Ephesians 2:18

Pray in the Spirit on all occasions.   Ephesians 6:18

We . . . worship by the Spirit of God.   Philippians 3:3

Prayer has often been compared to breathing.

With every breath we expel the impure air which would soon cause our death and inhale again the fresh air to which we owe our life. So we give out, in confession, the sins and, in petition, the needs and desires of our hearts. And in drawing in our breath again, we inhale the fresh air of the promises and the love and life of God in Christ. We do this through the Holy Spirit who is the breath of our life.

And this is because he is the breath of God. The Father breathes him into us to unite himself with our life. And then, just as inhaling follows exhaling, so God draws in again his breath and the Spirit returns to him laden with the desires and needs of our hearts.

Andrew Murray

Let the Spirit teach you how to pray. The more you pray, the more you will find yourself saying, 'I don't know how to pray.' Well, God understands that and has a plan to cover our need there. There is one who is a master intercessor. He understands praying perfectly. He is the Spirit of prayer. God sent him down to live inside us partly to teach us the fine art of prayer, so let him teach you.

S. D. Gordon

Nothing can be more foolish in prayer than to rush heedlessly into God's presence and ask the first thing that comes into our minds or that some thoughtless friend has asked us to pray for. When we first come into God's presence, we should be silent before him. We should look up to him to send his Holy Spirit to teach us how to pray. We must wait for the Holy Spirit and surrender ourselves to the Spirit; then we shall pray aright.

Often when we come to God in prayer, we do not feel like praying. What should we do? Stop praying until we do feel like it? Not at all. When we feel least like praying is the time when we most need to pray. We should wait quietly before God and tell him how cold and prayerless our hearts are, and look up to him and trust him to send the Holy Spirit to warm our hearts and draw them out in prayer. It will not be long before the glow of the Spirit's presence will fill our hearts and we will begin to pray with freedom, directness, earnestness and power. Many of the best seasons of prayer I have ever known have begun with a feeling of utter deadness and prayerlessness; but in my helplessness and coldness, I have cast myself upon God and looked to him to send his Holy Spirit to teach me to pray, and he has done it.

When we pray in the Spirit, we will pray for the right things in the right way. There will be joy and power.

R. A. Torrey

The prayer which prevails is that which is formed by the Holy Spirit. He is the medium of communication between heaven and earth; he reveals to us the thoughts and desires of God, so that we do not ask amiss. Prayer is transmitted from our hearts, borne forward by the Spirit and registered in the heart of the Lord. It is perhaps better to say that it originates there, is transmitted to us, and sent back from us to him.

F. B. Meyer

EFFECTIVE PRAYER

To pray with the understanding is easy and universal. We need to be reminded that, with the prayer of understanding, there must come prayer with the Spirit and prayer in the Holy Spirit. We need to give due place to each of the twofold operations of the Spirit. God's word must dwell in us richly; our faith must seek to hold it clearly and intelligently and to plead it in prayer. We must also remember that, in the inner sanctuary of our being, the Spirit prays for us what we do not know and cannot express.

Andrew Murray

It is clear that praying in the Spirit means much more than praying by the Spirit's help, although that is included. We pray by means of and in dependence on the Spirit's help, but the Spirit is the atmosphere in which the believer lives. So long as he is ungrieved, he is able to guide us in our petitions and create in us the faith that claims the answer. Our prayers will then be in substance the same as the intercessions of the Spirit within us.

Praying in the Spirit is praying along the same lines, about the same things and in the same name as the Holy Spirit.

J. Oswald Sanders[85]

There is no doubt that prayers in the Spirit will mean the cessation of a great many petitions. It is not an arrangement by which we obtain things which we personally desire. It is rather the provision through which we seek to be brought into conformity with the will of God and to obtain only the light which enables us to walk in it.

G. Campbell Morgan[86]

4
Effective Prayer
(Getting it right)
Part II

Right Attitudes (Approach with Care)

Being single minded and persistent ('I mean it!')

Ask and it will be given to you; seek and you will find; knock and the door will be opened to you. Matthew 7:7

Jacob replied, 'I will not let you go unless you bless me.' . . . The man said, 'Your name will no longer be Jacob but Israel, because you have struggled with God and with men and have overcome.'   Genesis 32:26, 28

[Jesus] left them and went away once more and prayed the third time, saying the same thing.   Matthew 26:44

Suppose one of you has a friend, and he goes to him at midnight and says, 'Friend, lend me three loaves of bread because a friend of mine on a journey has come to me, and I have nothing to set before him.' Then the one inside answers, 'Don't bother me. The door is already locked, and my children are with me in bed. I can't get up and give you anything.' I tell you, though he will not get up and give him the bread because he is his friend, yet because of the man's persistence he will get up and give him as much as he needs. So I say to you: Ask and it will be given you; seek and you will find; knock and the door will be opened to you. For everyone who asks receives; he who seeks finds; and to him who knocks, the door will be opened. Luke 11:5-10

Jesus told his disciples a parable to show them that they should always pray and not give up. He said, 'In a certain town there was a judge who neither feared God nor cared about men. And there was a widow in that town who kept coming to him with the plea, "Grant me justice against my adversary." For some time he refused. But finally he said to himself, ". . . Because this widow keeps bothering me, I will see that she gets justice, so that she won't eventually wear me out with her coming!" ' And the Lord said, 'Listen to what the unjust judge says. And will not God bring about justice for his chosen ones, who cry out to him day and night? . . . I tell you, he will see that they get justice, and quickly.' Luke 18:1-8

Prayer in its highest form and grandest success assumes the attitude of a wrestler with God. It is the contest, trial and victory of faith; a victory not secured from an enemy, but from him who tries our faith that he may enlarge it and tests our strength to make it stronger. Few things give such quickened and permanent vigour to the soul as a long exhaustive season of importunate prayer.

Our whole being must be in our praying; like John Knox, we must say and feel, 'Give me Scotland, or I die!' Our experience and revelations of God are born of our costly sacrifice, our costly conflicts, our costly praying. The wrestling, all night praying, of Jacob made an era never to be forgotten in Jacob's life, brought God to the rescue, changed Esau's attitude and conduct, changed Jacob's character, saved and affected his life and entered into the habits of a nation.

Prayer is a trade to be learned. We must be apprentices and serve our time at it. Painstaking care, much thought, practice and labour are required to be a skilful tradesman in praying. Practice in this, as well as in all other trades, makes perfect.

E. M. Bounds

No man is likely to do much good in prayer who does not begin by looking upon it in the light of work to be prepared for and persevered in with all the earnestness which we bring to bear on subjects which are, in our opinion, at once most interesting and most necessary.

Bishop Hamilton

God does not always give us what we ask in answer to the first prayer; he wants to train us and make us strong by compelling us to pray hard for the best things. He makes us *pray through*.

Many people call it submission to the will of God when God does not grant them their requests at the first or second asking. As a rule, this is not submission but spiritual laziness. We do not call it submission to the will of God when we give up after one or two efforts to obtain things by action; we call it lack of character. We should be careful about what we ask from God, but when we do begin to pray for a thing, we should never give up praying for it until we get it, or until God makes it very clear and very definite that it is not his will to give it.

Some would have us believe that it shows unbelief to pray twice for the same thing, that we ought to 'take it' the first time we ask. Doubtless there are times when we are able through faith in God's word or the leading of the Holy Spirit to claim the first time that which we have asked of God; but there are other times when we must pray again and again for the same thing before we get the answer. Those who have got beyond praying twice for the same thing, have got beyond their Master (Matthew 26:44). George Muller prayed for two men daily for over sixty years. One of these men was converted shortly before and the other shortly after Muller's death.

R. A. Torrey

Lukewarmness in prayer, as in everything else, is nauseating to God and comes away empty-handed. On the other hand, shameless persistence, the importunity that will not be denied, returns with the answer in its hands.

J. Oswald Sanders[87]

Elijah was clearly a passionate man, a man of strong feelings. There is tenderness as he carries the dead body of the child to his room (1 Kings 17:19); devotion to God's glory, when he cries out, 'I have been very zealous for the Lord God Almighty' (1 Kings 19:14). But he didn't rely on these feelings; he turned passion into prayer.

Strong feelings can be contagious, but we must learn to secure through God results which some try to achieve by the energy of their own nature. 'Elijah was a man just like us. He prayed earnestly that it would not rain, and it did not rain on the land for three and a half years. Again he prayed, and the heavens gave rain, and the earth produced its crops' (James 5:17, 18).

F. B. Meyer

The widow, in Jesus' parable (Luke 18:1-8), had no advocate to plead for her, so she was compelled to urge her own plea. To him the widow was a mere beggar, suing for a favour. Yet, because she was a beggar, he wished to be rid of her and there was only one way: to do as she wanted. He granted her request because in no other way could he silence or dismiss her.

The infinitely just Judge and good God is contrasted with this human judge. God's unspeakable love towards his people is in contrast to the indifference and utter selfishness of this earthly magistrate towards the widow. If the widow, in her situation, overcame by her persistence—how much more will the believer, who has the God of everlasting love and everlasting justice as his judge, and Jesus as his advocate and friend at court!

Like the unjust judge, the neighbour, in another parable of Jesus (Luke 11:5-10), finally yields to the demand of his neighbour; but he is not moved to do so by either friendship or sympathy; it is because he wants to be let alone and to have his rest and sleep unbroken that he gets up and gives the person what he needs. How much more will our heavenly Father, who loves us with unselfish, self-sacrificing and self-forgetting love, give bread to his needy children when they stand knocking at his gate!

In both parables, the message is clear: Don't give up; continue in prayer.

R. A. Torrey

Referring everything to God ('Be my constant companion').

. . . always pray and not give up. **Luke 18:1**

Be . . . faithful in prayer. **Romans 12:12**

Devote yourselves to prayer. **Colossians 4:2**

Pray in the Spirit on all occasions with all kinds of prayers and requests. **Ephesians 6:18**

Pray continually. **1 Thessalonians 5:17**

What do these verses mean? The minimum meaning is clear and very important: Pray very often. Make it a habit, the result of very many acts, to pray. In your praying, pass far beyond any limits of stated times. So set the Lord before you that it will be impossible to set a limit on your communion with him.

Every incident of life can be an opportunity for communicating with him. We are meant to talk with the Lord about everything: to confide in him, secretly and habitually, our sorrows and joys; our innermost thoughts and feelings. We are to look up to him in spiritual simplicity as each occasion of conversation or reading or memory or anticipation brings its problems. We are to talk with him about temptation, about the bliss of home, about the cross of solitude, about the snares of success and about the would-be stings of neglect, slander or disappointment.

A life kept in secret contact, in secret understanding, with Jesus Christ will diffuse a happy atmosphere of rest and purity.

But praying continually means more than praying very often. It also points to the deep union between the believer and his Lord; to his growing up into him in all things (Ephesians 4:15), so that he lives with the constant realisation that God is in all things and all things are in God. Such a realisation doesn't make articulate prayers unnecessary but it goes beyond them; it is like the soil from which they spring.

We need to discover this habitual life of prayer, hidden with Christ in God and, having discovered it, to explore it.

H. C. G. Moule

I will try not to put prayer alongside my work like a brother and sister standing side by side, but I would like to incorporate it in my work like the soul and the body. The relation of prayerfulness and work is not that of neighbours or contiguity, however close. Prayer and action are related as the feeling of pity is to the act of holding out your arms, as the decision to fight is to the hand that grasps the sword. Action is only the visible manifestation of the spirit of faith which motivates us.

Since God works with me and his invitation prompts and directs my good intentions, I do not need to leave my work to find him. Prayer should become part of my life like water moistening dust, or yeast which does not stay apart from the dough but is mixed with it.

Pierre Charles[88]

When a person is . . . spiritually dry, the answer can be a matter of repentance and patience. However, what of the Christian who feels empty for no apparent reason? Accept such dryness as from the very loving hand of God. He is asking us to meet him despite our feelings. Those children who come to him when they least feel like it would seem to me to be more precious to God than those who only make the effort when they are receiving showers of spiritual blessing. Spiritual dryness is simply God's way of saying, 'I trust you to be mine without having to work on your feelings. Thank you for loving me just out of your own personal commitment despite your feelings.'

Gary Strong[89]

It is taken for granted by some people that it is no good praying unless you feel like it. They believe that the worth of prayer depends on our emotional keenness at the time.

So far is that from being true that the precise opposite comes nearer the truth. Our prayers are more acceptable offered when we don't feel like it than when we do. Nor is it hard to understand why.

When we pray because we feel like it, we are pleasing ourselves. We want to pray and we do pray, and our prayer is acceptable to God in the degree that our will is in harmony with his.

But when we pray *not* feeling like it, we bring God not only the content of our prayer but also a disciplined spirit. We have kept our appointment with him against inclination. We have displeased ourselves in order to please him, and his pleasure is real indeed.

Feelings can be very sweet, and never to know the rapture of religion would be dreadful, but feelings are too insubstantial and too variable to be the guide to our praying. Feeling fluctuates with our health, our temperaments, the weather, the news; it fluctuates also with what we eat and who we last met.

W. E. Sangster[90]

Being definite and specific ('Here is my need.')

Give your servant success today by granting him favour in the presence of this man.   Nehemiah 1:11

Save me, I pray, from the hand of my brother Esau, for I am afraid he will come and attack me, and also the mothers with their children.   Genesis 32:11

O Lord, God of my master Abraham, give me success today, and show kindness to my master Abraham.
Genesis 24:12

Three times I pleaded with the Lord to take it [the thorn in the flesh] away from me.   2 Corinthians 12:8

Vague, waffling prayer is a waste of time and breath. To be effective, prayer must be on target. The Spirit can help us focus on one aspect of a mission enterprise 10,000 miles away, burdening us with the right request for that moment. Or he can motivate our hearts at any time of day or night to pray, and only after months do we learn how that prayer fitted into God's plan and how we were part of a vital prayer force in that intense spiritual battle.

Michael Baughen[91]

The background for special prayer in an emergency is the steady habit of daily prayer from which our knowledge of God grows. He who knows God in the intimacy gained from daily intercourse will not lack guidance when, in an emergency or faced by a weighty decision, he turns to him for special direction.

Donald Coggan[92]

Let your prayer be so definite that you can say as you leave the prayer room, 'I know what I have asked from the Father, and I expect an answer.'

Andrew Murray

We ought not to be content with general petitions. We ought to specify our wants before the throne of grace. It should not be enough to confess that we are sinners: we should name the sins of which our conscience tells us we are most guilty. It should not be enough to ask for holiness; we should name the graces in which we feel most deficient. It should not be enough to tell the Lord we are in trouble; we should describe our trouble and all its peculiarities.

This is what Jacob did when he feared his brother Esau. He told God exactly what it was that he feared. This is what Eliezer did, when he looked for a wife for his master's son. He spread before God precisely what he wanted. This is what Paul did when he had a thorn in the flesh. He pleaded with the Lord.

What should we think of the patient who told his doctor he was ill but never went into particulars?

What should we think of the wife who told her husband she was unhappy but did not specify the cause? What should we think of the child who told his father he was in trouble but nothing more? Christ is the true bridegroom of the soul, the true physician of the heart, the real father of all his people. Let us show that we feel this by being unreserved in our communications with him.

J. C. Ryle

Definite prayer teaches us to know our own needs better. It demands time and thought and self-scrutiny to find out what really is our greatest need. It searches us and puts us to the test as to whether our desires are honest and real. It leads us to judge whether our desires are according to God's word and whether we really believe that we shall receive the things we ask. It helps us to wait for the special answer and to recognise it when it comes.

And yet how much of our prayer is vague and pointless! Some cry for mercy but take not the trouble to know what mercy must do for them. Others ask, perhaps, to be delivered from sin but do not begin by bringing any sin by name from which the deliverance may be claimed. Still others pray for God's blessing on those around them, for the outpouring of God's Spirit on their land or the world, and yet have no special field where they wait and expect to see the answer. To all the Lord says: 'What is it now you really want and expect me to do?'

Each believer has his own circle: his family, friends and neighbours. If he were to take one or more of those by name, he would find that this really brings him in the training school of faith to personal and pointed dealing with his God.

Andrew Murray

Here is a kind of prayer that all who believe in prayer should seek to become skilled in: the brief, momentary, ejaculatory utterance of need. This may be called prayer in the form of a telegram; while the ordinary sort is in the letter form.

Because Nehemiah had formed the splendid habit of regular prayer, he found it only natural to adopt this method of emergency prayer. Sad as he was about the dreadful condition of his beloved city, and wondering however things could be put right, and how he himself could help towards it, the king suddenly shot the question at him: What do you want me to do? What a magnificent chance! What shall he ask for? How shall he use his opportunity? In all the excitement and possibility of the moment, he is man of God enough to see the utility of the sky-telegram. In such circumstances, the essential thing is swift action.

There was an emergency in Peter's life when he only had time for a telegram—circumstances demanded that he should carefully count and cut his words to the minimum—'Lord, save me' (Matthew 14:30).

Guy H. King[93]

A most beneficial exercise before the Father is to write things down so that I see exactly what I think and want to say.

It is a good thing to keep a note of things you prayed about when you were in distress. We remain ignorant of ourselves because we do not keep a spiritual autobiography.

Oswald Chambers

Praying in faith ('I believe!')

I tell you the truth, if you have faith as small as a mustard seed, you can say to this mountain, 'Move from here to there,' and it will move. Nothing will be impossible for you.   **Matthew 17:20, 21**

'Have faith in God,' Jesus answered. 'I tell you the truth, if anyone says to this mountain, "Go, throw yourself into the sea," and does not doubt in his heart but believes that what he says will happen, it will be done for him. Therefore I tell you, whatever you ask for in prayer, believe that you have received it, and it will be yours.'   **Mark 11:22–24**

The apostles said to the Lord, 'Lord, increase our faith.' He replied, 'If you have faith as small as a mustard seed, you can say to this mulberry tree, "Be uprooted and planted in the sea," and it will obey you.'

Luke 17:5, 6

God said, 'Let there be light,' and there was light.

Genesis 1:3

Before they call I will answer; while they are still speaking I will hear.   **Isaiah 65:24**

Faith's source and secret
Faith is the soul's organ of vision, hearing, feeling, by which we see, hear and 'handle' God. So the reality and power of all communion with God must hang on how far his word of promise is believed. To come into the place of prayer believing that he

is there and ready to give himself to the person who prays, is to receive an answer before we call and find him hearing while we are still speaking.

Jesus says, 'Have faith in God': literally, 'Have the faith of God.' This element is essential; it is as though God had said, 'Between you and me there can be no contact or communion until you believe in me, my existence and my readiness to reward your seeking.'

His comparison of faith to a grain of mustard seed must not be taken only to refer to the littleness of our faith. He commended the poor widow who put her two very small copper coins into the temple treasury not because of the small amount she put in but because she put in everything—all she had to live on (Mark 12:42–44). The mustard seed is small but it is hiding God's power and therefore represents the principle of life and so of growth, expansion and reproduction. Let the little mustard seed drop into the crevices of the rock and it can split the solid mass and heave it from its bed, by simple growth.

Faith is mighty, not because it's small, but because it is hiding God's power. It is the seed of God, having in it God's life, and where it lodges there is growth, movement, expansion and reproduction. In so far as it is genuine and godlike, it exercises the power of God and is irresistible.

Jesus speaks of faith being able to move mountains and mulberry trees. Why mountains and mulberry trees? The mountain suggests a massive obstacle—something which lies in the way and which can only be overcome with great difficulty and removed with even greater difficulty. The mulberry tree may be comparatively small but it has deep, fast-clinging roots that take hold of the soil and defy uprooting. It represents inward difficulties as the mountain represents outward obstacles. Faith is equal to both.

Faith can have authority. The master gives his servants his own power and entrusts them with authority to command. Faith claims not only blessing but power to bless. Faith in God so unites to God that it passes beyond the privilege of asking to the power of commanding. God said, 'Let there be light,' and there was light. And the disciple can also use the language of direction, of authority: 'Move from here to there.' 'Go, throw yourself into the sea.' In the spiritual realm there is one all-subduing, all-controlling force, power and energy: the Holy Spirit of God. Conform to the way the Spirit works and, in the work of God's hands, you may command the Spirit's power. As Coleridge wrote:

> Faith is an affirmation and an act.
> That bids eternal truth be fact.

A. T. Pierson

Faith is like a muscle which grows stronger and stronger with use, rather than rubber which can be stretched to almost any desired length. Overstrained faith is not pure faith, there is a mixture of the carnal element in it. There is no strain in the rest of faith. It asks for definite blessing as God may lead; it does not hold back through carnal timidity, nor press ahead too far through carnal eagerness.

I have definitely asked the Lord for several hundred families of Lisu believers. There are upwards of two thousand Lisu families in the district altogether. It might be said, 'Why do you not ask for a thousand?' I answer quite frankly, 'Because I have not faith for a thousand.' I have faith—or I would rather say, I believe the Lord has given me faith—for more than one hundred families but not for a thousand.

J. O. Fraser[94]

Faith in a faithful God
Our faith is the power with which we grasp God's power and make it ours.

Alexander McLaren

People say, 'Lord, increase our faith.' Did not the Lord rebuke his disciples for that prayer? He said, 'You do not want a great faith, but faith in a great God. If your faith were as small as a grain of mustard-seed, it would suffice to move this mountain!'

Hudson Taylor[95]

Faith is never mountain-moving because it moves mountains, but because it does not doubt God can move them, and will, at the need. Mountain-moving faith never tries, nor even thinks of trying, to move mountains. It is fully convinced it could not if it tried, but it is also confident it need not try, for God will do it.

'Great' faith is neither self-absorbed nor absorbed with circumstances but is all absorbed with God. For it recognises that its only duty is simply to roll its little insignificant mustard-seed self up against the foot of the tree, or mountain, and lie there, looking up to God, watching and waiting with confident expectation till he removes it.

G. B. Peck

All God's giants have been weak men, who did great things for God because they reckoned on his being with them.

We need a faith that rests on a great God, and which expects him to keep his own word and to do just what he has promised.

Every difficulty overcome by faith is 'bread'—strength and nourishment—to the child of God.

'They who trust him wholly/Find him wholly true'—but also when we fail to trust him fully he still remains unchangingly faithful. He is wholly true whether we trust him or not.

How many Christians go mourning, and lose joy, strength and opportunities of helping others, because they do not hold God's faithfulness! Holding his faithfulness, we may face with calm and sober but confident assurance of victory, every difficulty and danger.

Hudson Taylor[96]

Three phases of faith: In the first phase, we believe when there are favourable emotions; in the second, when there is absence of feeling; but in the third phase of faith, the person believes God and his word when circumstances, emotions, appearances, people and human reason all urge the contrary.

Anon

Faith in a mighty, creative God
There is a mighty ocean of power all around us, but for some reason we cannot tap it. It is like the electric current, which refuses to help us unless we have instruments precisely adapted to transmit the driving-power. Faith is absolutely necessary for the conveyance of God's power to meet the need and

sin and sorrow of the world. But when we find it deficient, when our heart believes not, when we find ourselves face to face with Jerichos that are closely shut, and with mountains that seem to mock the tiny levers with which we propose to move them, then we must turn to Christ and say: 'I trust you for faith, I trust you to keep me trusting: I do believe; help me overcome my unbelief!'

F. B. Meyer

It would appear that God acted on the principle of faith in the creation of the world. When he said to the non-existent light, 'Let there be light,' there was light. It is this same kind of creative faith we are called upon to exercise, the very faith of God. 'Now faith means . . . being certain of things we cannot see' (Hebrews 11:1, *Phillips*), and this conception opens to us a limitless realm of possibility.

J. O. Sanders[97]

All God's fullness will flow through the tiniest channel that faith opens out on his almighty power. Faith is the open heart towards him, and through the channel of faith Christ lives in and through us. Hudson Taylor heard God say: 'I am going to evangelise inland China and, if you will walk with me, I will do it through you.' D. L. Moody said that the beginning of his marvellous ministry was the remark made in his hearing: 'The world has yet to learn what God can do through a man wholly yielded to him.' It is not *what we do* but *what God does through us* that counts; and his mighty power, passing through the tiniest aperture of faith, keeps hollowing it wider.

F. B. Meyer

EFFECTIVE PRAYER

Beware in your prayers, above everything else, of limiting God, not only by unbelief, but by fancying that you know what he can do. Expect unexpected things—'above all that we ask or think'.

Each time, before you intercede, be quiet first and worship God in his glory. Think of what he can do and how he delights to hear the prayers of his redeemed people. Think of your place and privilege in Christ—and expect great things!

Andrew Murray

One of the most essential qualities of faith that is to attempt great things for God and expect great things from God, is holy audacity. Where we are dealing with a supernatural Being and taking from him things that are humanly impossible, it is easier to take much than little; it is easier to stand in a place of audacious trust than in a place of cautious, timid clinging to the shore. So, seamen in the life of faith, let us launch out into the deep and find that all things are possible with God, and all things are possible to him who believes.

A. B. Simpson

Prayer in faith—not faith in prayer
Prayer must be in faith. But please note that faith here is not believing that God *can* but that he *will*. It is kneeling and making the prayer, and then saying, 'Father, I thank you for this; that it will be so, I thank you'; then rising and going about your duties, saying, 'That thing is settled'; going again and again, repeating the prayer with thanks and then saying, as you go off, 'That matter is assured'; not going repeatedly to persuade God but because prayer is the deciding factor in a spiritual conflict

and each prayer is like a fresh broadside from your fleet upon the fort.

S. D. Gordon

We need to remember the distinction between *faith in prayer* and *prayer in faith*. Faith in prayer may be presumptuous and clamorous; it may present ultimatums to the Almighty demanding his acquiescence; it may try to make of prayer a magic demand of God. But prayer in faith asks everything in entire submission to the will of God. Prayer in faith rejoices in God's sovereignty, is confident that all forces are in his leash, and that to those who love him all things work together for good.

H. E. Fosdick[98]

God's omnipotence must be taken hold of by our faith and actually used, in deep humility but holy confidence, for the carrying through of his own great purpose.

If we could see what is behind the curtains of the invisible world, two streams of heavenly power would be distinctly visible: one an ascending line of prayer and the other a descending current of power. Such phenomena have actually been traced in innumerable instances. While Elijah was praying on Carmel, the clouds were actually marshalling on the distant horizon. While Jacob was praying at Peniel, the heart of Esau, as he lay in his tent that night, was going back to early memories and melting into the tender welcome which he was to give, later at noon, to his once-hated brother.

A. B. Simpson

Faith in God's promises

Faith is to prayer what the feather is to the arrow: without prayer it will not hit the mark.

We should cultivate the habit of pleading promises in our prayers. We should take with us some promise and say, 'Lord, here is your own word pledged. Do for us as you have said.' This was the habit of Jacob, Moses and David. Psalm 119 is full of things asked 'according to your word'.

Above all, we should cultivate the habit of expecting answers to our prayers. We should do like the merchant who sends his ships to sea. We should not be satisfied, unless we see some return.

J. C. Ryle

No matter how positive any promise of God's word may be, we will not enjoy it in actual experience unless we confidently expect its fulfilment in answer to our prayer. There must be confident, unwavering expectations.

But there is a faith that goes beyond expectation, that believes that the prayer is heard and the promise granted. This comes out in Mark 11:24: 'Whatever you ask for in prayer, believe that you have received it, and it will be yours.'

But how can we get this faith?

Let me say with emphasis that it cannot be pumped up. Many read this promise about the prayer of faith, then ask for things that they desire and try to make themselves believe that God has heard the prayer. This ends only in disappointment, for it is not real faith and the things are not granted. It is at this point that many make a collapse of faith altogether by trying to work up faith by an effort of their will; and, as the thing they made themselves believe they expected to get is not given, the very foundation of faith is often undermined.

So how does real faith come?

Romans 10:17 answers the question: 'Faith comes from hearing the message, and the message is heard through the word of Christ.' If we are to have real faith, we must study Scripture and find out what is promised, then simply believe the promises of God. Faith must have a warrant. Trying to believe something that you want to believe is not faith. Believing what God says is faith.

Also, faith comes through the Spirit. The Spirit knows the will of God and, if I pray in the Spirit and look to the Spirit to teach me God's will, he will lead me out in prayer along the line of that will and give me faith that the prayer is to be answered.

If there is no promise and no clear leading of the Spirit, there can be no real faith and there should be no upbraiding of self for lack of faith in such a case. But if the thing desired is promised in Scripture, we may well upbraid ourselves for lack of faith if we doubt; for we are making God a liar by doubting his word.

R. A. Torrey

Have faith in God, the living God. Let faith look to God more than to the thing promised: it is his love, his power, his living presence that will waken and work the faith. A doctor would say to someone asking for some means to get more strength into his arms and legs, that his whole constitution must be built up and strengthened. So the cure for a feeble faith is alone to be found in the invigoration of our whole spiritual life by communion with God.

Learn to believe God, to let God take possession of your life, and it will be easy to take hold of his promises. He who knows and trusts God, finds it easy to trust his promises too. God's promises will be to us what God himself is. It is the person who walks before the Lord and falls on his face to listen while the living God speaks to him, who will really receive the promises. Though we have God's promises in the Bible, with full liberty to take them, the spiritual power is lacking until God himself speaks them to us; and he speaks to those who walk and live with him.

Andrew Murray

The effects of faith

Prayer is faith resting in, acting with, leaning on and obeying God. Prayer is always believing. Faith must have a tongue by which it can speak. Prayer is the tongue of faith. Faith must receive. Prayer is the hand of faith stretched out to receive. Prayer must rise and soar. Faith must give prayer the wings to fly and soar. Prayer must have an audience with God. Faith opens the door, and access and audience are given. Prayer asks. Faith lays its hands on the things asked for.

E. M. Bounds

The prayer of faith is the power which converts promise into performance.

J. Oswald Sanders[99]

In human life, when we trust a man, we draw from him all that he is able to supply; in the divine life, faith draws upon the resources of God, so that they flow freely into our nature, and the results of our life-work are immensely increased.

Faith is possible amid a great deal of ignorance. It is clear that Gideon, Barak, Samson and Jephthah were ignorant of the truth which the gospel has revealed, and yet we learn that their work was largely due to their faith. Dispensations come and go; the revelation of God grows from less to more; but the attitude of faith is always the same—in the ordinary woman that touched the hem of Christ's garment, as in St John, the beloved disciple, who had years of training in Christ's 'school'.

Faith achieves very different results. In some it produces the heroic strength that turns the battle from the gate; in others, the suffering that endures the long ordeal of pain. Sometimes, it turns the edge of the sword, or shuts the mouths of lions. We know how electricity may be applied to all the various machinery of human life. In one place it is used for beaming light, in another to drive the car, or flash the message of music and speech from one continent to another. So faith is able to appropriate God's might for any purpose that lies within the compass of the life-task, whether active or passive.

F. B. Meyer

Doubt—a faith illness

Unbelief is something very different from doubt. Unbelief is an attribute of the will and consists of a person's refusal to believe; that is, refusal to see his own need, acknowledge his helplessness, go to Jesus and speak candidly and confidently with him about his sin and distress.

Doubt, on the other hand, is an anguish, a pain, a weakness, which at times affects our faith. We could therefore call it faith-distress, faith-anguish, faith-suffering, faith-tribulation. Such faith-illness can be more or less painful and more or less protracted, like other ailments. But if we can begin to look upon it as suffering which has been laid on us, it will lose its sting of distress and confusion.

O. Hallesby[100]

Helplessness and faith
The essence of faith is to come to Christ. This is the first and the last and the surest indication that faith is still alive. Faith manifests itself clearly and plainly when a sinner, instead of fleeing from God and his own responsibility, as he did before, comes into the presence of Christ with all his sin and distress. The sinner who does this believes.

Notice the simple but unmistakable mark of a living faith. Such a faith as this sees its own need, acknowledges its own helplessness, goes to Jesus, tells him just how bad things are, and leaves everything with him.

You and I can now tell how much faith we need in order to pray. We have faith enough when we in our helplessness turn to Jesus. This shows us clearly that true prayer is a fruit of helplessness and faith. Helplessness becomes prayer the moment that you go to Jesus and speak candidly and confidently with him about your needs.

O. Hallesby[101]

Why is prayer so startlingly effective when we admit our helplessness? First, because God insists on our facing up to the true facts of our human situation. Thus we lay under our prayer structure the firm foundation of truth rather than self-delusion or wishful thinking.

This recognition and acknowledgment of our helplessness is also the quickest way to that right attitude which God recognises as essential to prayer. It deals a mortal blow to the most serious sin of all—man's independence that ignores God.

Another reason is that we cannot learn first-hand about God—what he is like, his love for us as individuals and his real power—so long as we are relying on ourselves and other people. And fellowship with Jesus is the true purpose of life and the only foundation for eternity. It is real, this daily fellowship which he offers us.

So if your every human plan and calculation has miscarried, if, one by one, human props have been knocked out and doors have shut in your face, take heart. God is trying to get a message through to you, and the message is: 'Stop depending on inadequate human resources. Let me handle the matter.'

Here are three suggestions for presenting him with the prayer of helplessness.

First, be honest with God. Tell him that you are aware of the fact that in his eyes you are helpless. Give God permission to make you feel your helplessness *at the emotional level*, if that's what he wants. And recognise that this may be painful. There is a good psychological reason as to why this first step is necessary. Unless the power of our emotions is touched, it is as if a fuse remains unlit.

Second, take your heart's desire to God. You have your helplessness. Now grip with equal strength of will your belief that God can do through you what you cannot do. It may seem to you for a time that you are relying on emptiness, dangling over a chasm. Disregard these feelings and quietly thank God that he is working things out.

Third, watch now for opening doors. When the right door opens, you will have a quiet inner assurance that God's hand is on the knob.

Catherine Marshall[102]

Being confident ('Your gentleness has made me great.')

Let us ... approach the throne of grace with confidence, so that we may receive mercy and find grace to help us in our time of need.   **Hebrews 4:16**

'Present your case,' says the Lord. 'Set forth your arguments,' says Jacob's King.   **Isaiah 41:21**

Moses sought the favour of the Lord his God. 'O Lord,' he said, 'why should your anger burn against your people, whom you brought out of Egypt with great power and a mighty hand? Why should the Egyptians say, "It was with evil intent that he brought them out, to kill them in the mountains and wipe them off the face of the earth"? Turn from your fierce anger; relent and do not bring disaster on your people. Remember your servants Abraham, Isaac and Israel, to whom you swore by your own self: "I will make your descendants as numerous as the stars in the sky and I will give your descendants all his land I promised them, and it will be their inheritance for ever." Then the Lord relented and did not bring on his people the disaster he had threatened.   **Exodus 32:11–14**

Joshua said, 'Ah, Sovereign Lord, why did you ever bring this people across the Jordan to deliver us into the hands of the Amorites to destroy us ... O Lord, what can I say, now that Israel has been routed by its enemies? The Canaanites and the other people of the country will hear about this and they will surround us and wipe out our name from the earth. What then will

you do for your own great name?'   **Joshua 7:7–9**

Jabez cried out to the God of Israel, 'Oh that you would bless me and enlarge my territory!' ... And God granted his request.   **1 Chronicles 4:10**

God delights to respond to daring prayer. How quickly he responded to the audacity of the Syrophoenician woman though her prayer had no right of claim (Mark 7:24–30). He encourages us to ask freely for the impossible as for the possible, since to him all difficulties are the same size—less than himself.

There is an ambition in prayer which is well-pleasing to God. He is not honoured by the presenting of minimum requests. Because we are coming to the throne of a great king, we should honour him by bringing worthy petitions. Granting them will not strain his resources.

Jabez is an example of ambitious praying. He would be content with no ordinary blessing from the hand of God. He appealed for an extension of his boundaries. He was not content to fill a little space for God when he could fill a big one. The unselfishness and purity of his motives is guaranteed by the answer granted.

J. Oswald Sanders[103]

Being humble and reverent ('I bow in your awesome presence.')

God opposes the proud but gives grace to the humble.
James 4:6

I live in a high and holy place, but also with him who is contrite and lowly in spirit, to revive the spirit of the

lowly and to revive the heart of the contrite.

Isaiah 57:15

Hallowed be your name.   **Matthew 6:9**

Guard your steps when you go to the house of God. Go near to listen rather than to offer the sacrifice of fools, who do not know when they do wrong. Do not be quick with your mouth, do not be hasty in your heart to utter anything before God. God is in heaven and you are on earth, so let your words be few.   **Ecclesiastes 5:1, 2**

Jesus teaches humility by a most dramatic and striking contrast between the Pharisee and the tax-collector (Luke 18:9–14). There are thirty-four words in the Pharisee's prayer but there is not a word of adoration, confession or supplication among them, and the word 'I' comes four times; it is all self-congratulation under the pretence of thanksgiving. The Pharisee may have been all that he affirmed—a man of clean outward life–but it is very plain that he was puffed up with pride: blinded and dazzled not by the glory of God but by his own superior excellence; and that he knew nothing about drawing near to God, because no one can do that without gaining a new insight into his own inner corruption, just as in the glare of the midday sun nothing seems clean.

The tax collector may have been everything that the Pharisee thanked God he was not. Tax collectors had ample opportunity to levy a tax greater than the government authorised for personal gain and they generally did so. But whatever the guilt of the tax collector, the redeeming feature is that he knew and felt it. Physically he stood at a distance; in reality he was much the nearer of the two to God's presence. He beat his breast and found the courage to speak one short sentence but in it were conveyed adoration, confession and supplication.

Conviction of sin, deep, abiding and prostrating, is not only very rare but it indicates a ripeness of Christian character. The nearer we get to God by grace, the more we feel our distance by nature.

It requires a trained eye to see minute defects and detect slight blemishes. A painting that an undisciplined observer thinks is a superb work of art, the educated artist may condemn as a worthless daub—not because he is hypercritical but because he has a higher and truer conception of accuracy in drawing, skill in colouring and so forth. Michelangelo had so studied anatomy that he could detect the least error in the proportions of the human form on canvas. So it does not follow, because I seem to myself to be a far worse sinner than I did when I first found Jesus, that I *am* a worse one; it may be that I am far more like God but have learned to detect sin where I once saw none, just as the painting becomes a daub not because it has changed but because the eye scanning it has. The Pharisee looked at himself and saw nothing to condemn and much to applaud; the tax collector, looking at himself, saw nothing to approve and everything to condemn and abhor. However great the difference in the two characters, the greater difference was in the eyes that looked at them; in the one case blinded by self-righteous pride, in the other opened to see the hatefulness of sin.

Don't be surprised, child of God, as you seek to draw near to and be like God, if your sense of sin becomes more intolerable. Thank God that you see clearly; only don't stop with a look at yourself; look away to Jesus and ask that you may know him and lose even the sense and sight of your sin in the sense and sight of your Saviour.

A. T. Pierson

Prayer must be reverent. The tenderest words, the simplest confidences, the closest intimacy will be welcomed and reciprocated by our Father in heaven. But we must remember that he is the great king, and his name is holy. Angels veil their faces in his presence. There should be constant remembrance that in prayer we stand in the presence-chamber of the great creator, preserver and ruler of the universe.

F. B. Meyer

God has invited us to come freely into his presence but we must realise that we are still coming before God. When confronted with the Lord God Omnipotent himself, who would speak as if to a friend at a football match? We may come boldly but never arrogantly, never presumptuously, never flippantly, as if we were dealing with a peer.

R. C. Sproul[104]

Dance if you want before the Lord Jehovah. Sing his praises with an abandoned joy. Be merry in his presence and clap your hands. Let your guitars sound their melodies and your castanets their rhythm. Stomp your feet and sway your body.

But remember you are in the presence of the Most High God. He gives you breath. He holds your pulsing heart between his fingers. His rage against evil will never cease. It does not harm you because in your case it is assuaged by the blood of his only Son. And for his sake he welcomes you with love. Let your rejoicing then be with reverence and with godly fear.

John White[105]

Being in accord with others ('United we stand.')

They raised their voices together in prayer to God.
Acts 4:24

Make my joy complete by being like-minded, having the same love, being one in spirit and purpose.
Philippians 2:2

The symphony of prayer in which believers unite is not merely the result of an agreement with each other. Such agreement is only effective when it is the result of the Holy Spirit's own working—bringing disciples into harmony first with himself and then with each other. The picture suggested is that of music. Praying people are like the keyboard of a big musical instrument in tune with the mind and purpose of God. The Holy Spirit, the divine musician, like a true artist, lays his hands on one or more keys, which he has first brought into harmony with God's will and with one another, to make a perfect chord, so that God hears both the melody of acceptable individual prayer and the harmony of acceptable joint prayer.

We cannot arbitrarily agree about anything we ask for (Matthew 18:19); only as we first agree with the Holy Spirit, so that our prayer becomes the expression of God's will, can there be the right kind of agreement with each other. In other words, sympathy with God must be the basis of symphony among disciples. The Holy Spirit is able to bring people into spiritual accord. One day we will undoubtedly find that praying disciples, far apart and unknown to one another, have been led by the Spirit into simultaneous and sympathetic prayer for the same blessings, praying at the same time for the same things, because the same Spirit has been moving in their hearts and interceding in and through them.

A. T. Pierson

To be at odds with another Christian is to frustrate the prayer of Jesus. This is why disunity grieves God so much. Jesus prays at this moment for our unity, that we might be at one with each other. Whenever we realise that we are not at one with other Christians, we are working against Jesus at prayer. Let this thought spur us into getting right with each other.

The oneness for which Jesus prays for you and me is the same oneness in which the Father and the Son live. Bring before God relationships in your family and in your local fellowship and hear again Jesus praying: 'I pray . . . that all of them may be one, Father, just as you are in me and I am in you' (John 17:20, 21).

James Jones[106]

Corporate prayer often needs good leadership by those who are sensitive to the Spirit. It may be helpful to start with a time of worship, consciously lifting our minds and hearts from ourselves to the Lord. Too many prayers are earthbound. We are to set our minds on things above, encouraging one another to know that the Lord is with us. We need to raise the level of corporate faith and expectancy.

Short bursts of praise and prayer from as many as possible are far better than the long prayers of the 'professionals'. Such perorations may impress some like-minded saints, but they will kill most prayer meetings. Encourage sensitivity both to the Spirit and to one another. It helps when one theme at a time is 'prayed through' rather than jumping randomly from one topic to another. We have a New Testament model for such gatherings: everyone should have some contribution, each bringing different gifts to glorify Christ and to strengthen his Body (1 Corinthians 14:26).

David Watson[107]

5

The Range of God's Answers

(Answers come in all shapes and sizes)

Astonished by his answer, they became silent.
Luke 20:26

'Where do you come from?' [Pilate] asked Jesus, but Jesus gave him no answer.
John 19:9

In the day of my trouble I will call to you, for you will answer me.
Psalm 86:7

Moses spoke and the voice of God answered him.
Exodus 19:19

[David] called on the Lord, and the Lord answered him with fire from heaven on the altar of burnt offering.
1 Chronicles 21:26

Elijah was a man just like us. He prayed earnestly that it would not rain, and it did not rain on the land for

three and a half years. Again he prayed, and the heavens gave rain, and the earth produced its crops.
James 5:17, 18

The Lord said, 'Go out and stand on the mountain in the presence of the Lord, for the Lord is about to pass by.' Then a great and powerful wind tore the mountains apart and shattered the rocks before the Lord, but the Lord was not in the wind. After the wind there was an earthquake, but the Lord was not in the earthquake. After the earthquake came a fire, but the Lord was not in the fire. And after the fire came a gentle whisper. When Elijah heard it, he pulled his cloak over his face and went out and stood at the mouth of the cave. Then a voice said to him, 'What are you doing here, Elijah?'
1 Kings 19:11–13

Is not this the kind of fasting I have chosen: to loose the chains of injustice and untie the cords of the yoke, to set the oppressed free and break every yoke? Is it not to share your food with the hungry and to provide the poor with shelter . . .? Then you will call, and the Lord will answer; you will cry for help, and he will say: Here am I.
Isaiah 58:6, 7, 9

When any Israelite sets up idols in his heart and puts a wicked stumbling-block before his face and then goes to a prophet, I the Lord will answer him myself in keeping with his great idolatry. I will do this to recapture the hearts of the people of Israel, who have all deserted me for their idols.
Ezekiel 14:4, 5

O Lord our God, you answered them; you were to Israel a forgiving God, though you punished their misdeeds.
Psalm 99:8

A God Who Answers

Before they call I will answer; while they are still speaking I will hear. **Isaiah 65:24**

In my anguish I cried to the Lord, and he answered by setting me free. **Psalm 118:5**

In your distress you called and I rescued you, I answered you out of a thundercloud; I tested you at the waters of Meribah. **Psalm 81:7**

Every prayer of the Christian, made in faith, according to the will of God, for that which God has promised, offered up in the name of Jesus Christ, and under the influence of his Spirit, whether for temporal or spiritual blessings, is, or will be, fully answered.

E. Bickersteth

One thing is sure: Jesus wants us to count on the certainty that asking, seeking and knocking cannot be in vain. Receiving an answer, finding God, and the opened heart and home of God, are the certain fruits of prayer.

The more carefully we gather together what Jesus spoke on prayer, the clearer it becomes that he wishes us to think of prayer simply as the means to an end, and of the answer as proof that we and our prayer are acceptable to the Father in heaven. Not that Christ wants us to count the gifts of higher value than the fellowship and favour of the Father. But the Father means the answer to be the token of his favour and of the reality of our fellowship with him.

A life marked by daily answers to prayer is the

proof of our spiritual maturity; that we are truly abiding in Christ; that our will is at one with God's will; that our faith has grown strong to see and take what God has prepared for us. Prayer is very blessed; the answer is more blessed still, being the response from the Father that our prayer, our faith and our will are as he would wish them to be.

Andrew Murray

Even when God cannot answer affirmatively a person's petition, he can answer the person. Paul's petition for relief from his physical distress was not affirmatively answered, but Paul was answered. He went out from the denied request, three times repeated, with a reply from God that put fortitude and courage into him: 'My grace is sufficient for you, for my power is made perfect in weakness' (2 Corinthians 12:9). God always answers true prayer in one of two ways—'No good prayer ever comes weeping home.' For either he changes the circumstances or he gives sufficient power to overcome them; he answers either the petition or the person.

H. E. Fosdick[108]

If we only take as answers those that are visible to our senses, we are in a very elementary condition of grace.

Oswald Chambers

It will be a wonderful moment for some of us when we stand before God and find that the prayers we clamoured for in early days and imagine were never answered, have been answered in the most amazing ways, and that God's silence has been the sign of the answer. If we always want to be able to point to something and say, 'This is the way God answered my prayers,' God cannot trust us yet with his silence.

Some prayers are followed by silence because they are wrong, others because they are bigger than we can understand.

Oswald Chambers

Watch for the answers

Wait for the Lord; be strong and take heart and wait for the Lord. **Psalm 27:14**

How difficult it is for us to wait on and for God! We are so impatient, so activist. 'The trouble is that God is not in a hurry, and I am' (William Booth). We need to learn that all really effective action begins in quietly waiting for God to work—and then putting our efforts into working with him.

James Graham[109]

When a person is talking to someone who does not listen to him, he will stop speaking. So will God if we do not listen for his answers. What is said about faith—'You need to persevere so that when you have done the will of God, you will receive what he has promised' (Hebrews 10:36)—can also be said of prayer. It is not enough to pray; after you have prayed, you need to listen for an answer so that you may receive your prayers. If you do not observe God's answers, how will you be able to bless him and thank him for hearing your prayers?

John Bunyan

'I will stand at my watch and station myself on the ramparts; I will look to see what he will say to me' (Habakkuk 2:1). I am convinced that we lose many answers to our prayers not because we do not pray but because we do not go up to our tower to watch for and welcome God's answers to our prayers. 'Why should I answer him?' God might say. 'He is never on watch when I send my answer. When they reach his house and heart, he takes them, regarding them as common and everyday things. He never wonders at my grace to him. He holds a thousand of my benefits but does not seem to know it.' I am sure that we would get far more, and far more wonderful, answers to prayer if only we were far more on the lookout for them.

Alexander Whyte

Receive the Answers

Everyone who asks receives.   **Matthew 7:8**

Much of our prayer fails because we forget that Jesus said, 'Whatever you ask for in prayer, believe that you have *received* it, and it will be yours' (Mark 11:24).

The sequence is something like this: The person kneels before God, glorifying and praising him for his greatness and goodness. He is conscious of needing some very special gift which is promised. In the name of Christ, he presents the request with the confidence of a child. Earnestly, he unfolds the reason why the gift is so necessary. But he does not leave prayer at this point and go away in uncertainty as to what will happen. By an act of the spirit, the person receives, and realises that he has

154

received, the spiritual or even temporal gift: that special grace for which he asked—to be discovered and used under stress of need—or that temporal gift, though it may be kept back until the precise moment when it can be delivered, in much the same way as a present can be bought long before the time of handing it to the person to whom it is to be given (see 1 Samuel 1:15, 18, 27).

This is what Christ meant by receiving and it has a mighty effect on prayer because it makes it so much more definite. It leads to praise as we thank God for his gift. We must *take* as well as pray.

F. B. Meyer

How God Answers

The Lord answered Job out of the storm. He said: Who is this that darkens my counsel with words without knowledge? Brace yourself like a man; I will question you, and you shall answer me.   Job 38:1, 2

Does God really tell us things when we pray? Yes. We shall probably not hear voices, nor feel sudden strong impressions of a message coming through (and we should be wise to suspect such experiences should they come our way); but as we analyse and verbalise our problems before God's throne, and tell him what we want and why we want it, and think our way through passages and principles of God's written word bearing on the matter in hand, we shall find many certainties crystallising in our hearts as to God's view of us and our prayers and his will for us and others. If you ask, 'Why is this or that happening?' no light may come, for 'the secret things belong to the Lord our God' (Deuteronomy

29:29); but if you ask, 'How am I to serve and glorify God here and now, where I am?' there will
always be an answer.

J. I. Packer[110]

God speaks in the spirit of man and those who
meditate long on holy things learn how to dis-
entangle the voice of God from all the other voices
which speak inside us. Memory, fear, hope . . . all
of them talk in turn and sometimes they all talk
together! It's pandemonium let loose.

But, in those whose joy over the years it has been
to think on God, another voice awakes on occasion,
as quiet as some of the others are strident and bearing a strange assurance with it. This voice does not
argue or bleat or natter. It speaks with authority
and makes you certain that this isn't you. It is an
awesome experience and leaves one in no doubt
that God does speak in the spirit of man.

It isn't only to prophets and saints that he speaks.
With enough faith to listen and enough patience to
persist, *you* might hear this voice—personal, penetrating and deeply persuasive.

'But any maniac could claim to hear the voice of
God,' the incredulous will say. Of course. We know
that also. That is why we check the guidance which
comes from the voice within by the likeness of God
revealed in Jesus Christ.

W. E. Sangster

How does one put oneself in the way of receiving
guidance from God?

You are in the spirit of prayer, withdrawn from
the world. You are in the conscious presence of
God. Self is no longer at the centre. You see things

differently because you see them in the light of God. Conscience is at its tenderest. Spiritual perception is sharp and penetrating. It is God and you.

Listen! Something comes—clearly, maybe, or not so clear. If it is something to do, make a note of it and get it done as soon as possible; a letter to write, a call to make, an apology, possibly.

If you feel uncertain whether what comes to you in the quietness is of God, test it by its harmony with all that you know of Jesus and discuss it in confidence with some wise and keen Christian friend. God's guidance does run counter at times to our best judgment. Paul's fine judgment directed him once to Bithynia but the Spirit stayed him and God called him (against his judgment!) to Macedonia, to Europe—and to us.

W. E. Sangster[111]

How do God's messages come? Often in the language of Scripture. God selects a text or passage we have known for years and makes it radiate with a new light. It is as though he says, 'This is the relevant word for you now!' Sometimes it is a couplet from the hymn book or a chapter in a modern book of devotion or a phrase from a praying friend. But we know it by the different, shining, commanding quality. It is as though God says, 'This is it.'

Sometimes God borrows our own tongue and talks to us. How wonderful these secret conversations of the soul can be! The greatest spiritual hours of my life have been in these conversations. You raise a question with God and go on talking of your perplexity, and he seems to take over, asking you questions and elucidating answers which were sometimes inside you already and sometimes come direct from him. You get to the point where you hardly know who is asking and who is answering, but it doesn't matter. The session ends leaving you lost in wonder, love and praise. You can go on a long time on the memory of one such exalted hour. Should the time come in which God seems for a while not to answer, you can say in complete trust, 'I have heard God speak. I can bear his silence. He will speak again when he is ready.'

W. E. Sangster[112]

God is constantly seeking to meet us in the common and unexpected moments of life. He does not wait for what we are pleased to call the 'grand moments' but he will make the commonplace the grand. We walk about blind to the glory that is around us because we do not expect to find it there. We mortgage the joys of the present, the quiet homely joys of humdrum days, to our anticipations of some distant time of overwhelming happiness of the kind that never comes to most people.

W. E. Sangster[113]

What God 'says'

Heaven is my throne and the earth is my footstool. Where is the house you will build for me? Where will my resting-place be? Has not my hand made all these things, and so they came into being? . . . This is the one I esteem: he who is humble and contrite in spirit, and trembles at my word.'   **Isaiah 66:1, 2**

'Yes' and 'No' are not the only possible answers to prayer. 'Yes, but not your way,' is a third ... A fourth answer ... is, 'Yes, but not yet.'

Leith Samuel[114]

Perhaps you ask, 'How can I know whether my prayers have been answered or not?' Sometimes the case is so obvious that it cannot be mistaken: Jehoshaphat prays and he is rescued from his enemies; Hezekiah prays and he is rescued from illness; Jonah prays and he is rescued from the belly of the whale; the church prays and Peter is rescued from Herod. The following, among many others, are more examples of answers to particular requests: Genesis 25:21; 1 Chronicles 5:20; 2 Chronicles 33:13; Ezra 8:23.

At other times prayers are answered rather in the increase of grace to bear affliction than in its removal, as in the case of Paul's thorn in the flesh.

There are at least four ways in which God answers prayers: by giving the things prayed for at the time (Daniel 9:23); by suspending the answer for a time and giving it afterwards (Luke 18:7); by withholding the mercy for which you ask but giving you a much better mercy in place of it (Deuteronomy 3:24; 34:4, 5); by giving you patience to bear the loss of the answer you wanted (2 Corinthians 12:9).

When your prayers are *not* answered as you would wish, let it lead you to self-examination. Perhaps the prayer has been answered in a way you had not thought of. Perhaps you were wanting something that would only have encouraged pride or were only considering ease and comfort, without any thought of spiritual edification. Or look for the cause in your neglect of Christ's intercession, or your ingratitude for former answers. Question your own faith, the fervour of your desires, the purity of your purpose, your manner of asking; question anything rather than God's faithfulness: 'Let God be true, and every man a liar' (Romans 3:4). Also, God will not answer those who have an idol in their hearts or are continuing with some habitual sin (Isaiah 59:2; Ezekiel 14:13).

When your prayers *are* answered in the way you wish, let it assure you of God's faithfulness and love; encourage you to renew your prayers, to seek God more constantly, to depend more simply on his strength, to give yourself more completely to him and never to fear doing anything for him; excite you to abound in thanksgiving and praise.

E. Bickersteth

Yes

No matter how many promises God has made, they are 'Yes' in Christ. And so through him the 'Amen' is spoken by us to the glory of God.   2 Corinthians 1:20

There is a realm in the Christian life where God never says, 'No.' He never says 'No,' to your persistent and eager request that he will make you like his Son.

Raymond Ortlund[115]

The most important thing about all prayer is not its words, its form, its length, its fervour, but its quality; and the most important thing about its quality is that it should rise from a spirit wholly Christ-like. To such prayer, the father's ear is always open.

R. E. O. White[116]

How old must we be before we begin to realise that prayer can't get us everything we want unless the thing we want is right for us to have?

Name withheld[117]

Yes—and more than you've asked for

The ability of God is beyond our prayers, beyond our largest prayers! Sometimes I have thought that my asking was too presumptuous, it was even beyond the power of God to give. And yet Paul spoke of God as the one who is able to give more than we can ask or imagine. I have asked for a cupful, and the ocean remains. I have asked for a sunbeam and the sun still shines. My best asking falls immeasurably short of my Father's giving. It is beyond all that we ask.

J. H. Jowett

Yes—if you play your part

Some prayers are conditional. God's answer cannot be assumed until the condition is fulfilled. Repeatedly and clearly, Jesus insists, for example, that unless a person forgives his brother, his own plea for pardon will not be heard. Also, the prayer for fruitfulness cannot be answered to those who fail to 'remain in the vine' for 'apart from me you can do nothing' (John 15:4, 5). There are many other examples of promises in Scripture based on conditions—not because we must first of all deserve the blessing but because some preparation of ourselves is essential to making the blessing possible.

The second kind of conditional prayer depends on the willingness of others. We are called to intercede for others but God made them free to disobey, to fall, to resist his grace and, ultimately, to be lost. Jesus prayed for Peter—but Peter still denied him. Even his intercession could not evade the test or prevent the fall. Yet the prayer of Jesus must have entered into the total experience of Peter and, together with the warning and the look, helped to melt his heart and make him penitent. But Peter's freedom of spiritual development is part of the will of God within which all prayer is set and his experience was not to be miraculously sidestepped. Our prayers for others can intensify the spiritual forces playing on them for good and can surround them with protective care and love. But God will not and, if he is to remain consistent, cannot save the unwilling heart.

R. E. O. White[118]

Yes—but not yet

So often when we pray to our heavenly Father about something affecting our lives or the lives of others, the Father says, 'Yes, of course, let's enjoy this together.' We rejoice in the answer to prayer, and in the sense of his presence and blessing.

Yet there will be times when some greater purpose has to be the deciding factor and when our request must be put on one side or its answer delayed. Zechariah and Elizabeth learned this lesson (Luke 1). Their longing for a child must often have been on their lips in prayer. There seems to have been nothing in them to prevent their prayer being answered; they were both upright in the sight of God, observing all the Lord's commandments and regulations blamelessly (verse 6). The explanation for the delay was that that God had chosen Elizabeth to bear John the Baptist as a son. As a herald of the appearance of Christ, the timing of John's birth was all-important. He was a vital part of the greater purposes of the Lord.

Michael Baughen[119]

You pray dishonestly when you say to God things that you do not mean, when you feign an interest in his business or when you conceal your real desires under your pious reference to God's will. The result of dishonesty in prayer is almost always delay in God's answer. Just as parents insist that their children ask properly or say please, so God sometimes says to his children, 'I know what you want but, before I give it to you, let's be a little clearer about why you want it and how you are asking.' And since God's timing is always perfect, he may delay the answer to show you the dishonesty of your mind and motives rather than win your easy devotion by doing just what you asked the first time.

John Paterson

The angel waited till Jacob could wrestle no more, being completely exhausted; and then he blessed him. Jesus waited until the woman fell at his feet saying, 'Lord, help me!' so that he could give her what she asked. He waited to be gracious till the apostles and others had reached such a condition of helplessness that he could give them their Pentecost.

Too often we misunderstand God's dealings with us. When he delays, we conclude that he is neglecting us; in fact, he is waiting, at no small cost to himself, until we come to the end of ourselves and the way is clear for him to work a more astounding miracle than we had dared to hope for.

God's delays are not denials; they are not neglectful or unkind. He is waiting for precisely the right moment to pour out his blessings on us.

F. B. Meyer

Some things God cannot give to a person until he has prepared and proved his spirit by persistent prayer. Such praying cleans the house, cleanses the windows, hangs the curtains, sets the table, opens the door, until God says, 'The house is ready. Now the guest may come in.'

H. E. Fosdick[120]

There may be some prayers which you must be content never to see answered in this world; such as, perhaps, prayers for the downfall of God's enemies and the flourishing of the gospel. Such prayers are not lost but will have answers. If they are the work of the Spirit of Christ, made to God in his name, they are eternally accepted and of eternal force and therefore may be answered in after ages.

John Bunyan

It would not be difficult to find two Christians who agree that ridding the world of cancer or wars would be a good idea. Their prayer in this matter would not automatically accomplish their desire. The word of God indicates that wars, poverty and disease will be present at the time of Christ's return. To expect their absolute elimination before the appointed time is to grasp prematurely the future promises of God. What life will be like in heaven would be delightful to us now, but all our prayers cannot force God to give us this future situation in this present world.

We still must suffer the ravages of sin, disease and death. We entreat God to comfort us, to deliver us, to heal us—but we cannot demand these things in an absolute way.

The idea that God 'always wills healing' has been a destructive distortion in the Christian community. The pastoral problems emanating from this are enormous.

R. C. Sproul[121]

Yes—but not in your way
Not every prayer we offer is answered exactly as we want it to be. If it were, we would be dictating to God, and prayer would degenerate into a mere system of begging. Just as an earthly father knows what is best for his children's welfare, so God takes into consideration the particular needs of his human family and meets them out of his wonderful storehouse. If we ask according to his will, and for his glory, the answers will come in ways that will astonish us and fill our hearts with songs of thanksgiving. God is a rich and bountiful father and he does not forget his children or withhold from them anything which it would be to their advantage to receive.

J. Kennedy Maclean

In asking for spiritual blessings, for repentance, faith, humility, holiness and love, we are sure of having the particular request granted, for 'it is God's will that you should be holy' (1 Thessalonians 4:3). Yet in these things the way of granting the request may, at first sight, seem like a denial.

We pray for increase of faith, patience or other

Christian graces; and our trials, instead of being removed, seem greatly aggravated. The clouds grow darker and darker. But with the secret support of the Holy Spirit, we do not sink under our burden. And, in the midst of all these trials, the very things which we asked for are given. There is no exercise for faith when all is smooth; no room for patience when there is no suffering; the graces which we wanted need difficulties, sorrows and trials in order to be shown, exercised and granted.

E. Bickersteth

God's way of answering the Christian's prayer for more patience, experience, hope and love is often to put him into the furnace of affliction.

Richard Cecil

> I asked for strength, that I might achieve,
> I was made weak, that I might learn humbly to obey.
> I asked for health, that I might do greater things,
> I was given infirmity, that I might do better things.
> I asked for riches, that I might be happy,
> I was given poverty, that I might be wise.
> I asked for power, that I might have the praise of men,
> I was given weakness, that I might feel the need of God.
> I asked for all things, that I might enjoy life,
> I was given life, that I might enjoy all things,
> I got nothing that I asked for—but everything I had hoped for.
> Almost despite myself, my unspoken prayers

were answered,
I am, among all men, most richly blest.

Anon

There is more than one way to move a mountain. The New Testament stresses that God loves to use weak vessels (people) to do his work so that he, not they, will get the glory. And in the light of all the spiritual benefits resulting from sickness and suffering, God may choose that our very sickness be his way of moving the mountains before us.

As we grow in our faith, our way of looking at things changes. Once it seemed as if the only way God could glorify himself would be to remove our sufferings. Now it becomes clear that he can glorify himself through our sufferings.

Joni Eareckson[122]

Yes—but you won't like it!
Men are given to complaining of *unanswered* prayer but the great disasters are due to *answered* prayers. The trouble with men is that so often they do get what they want. When the prodigal in the far country came to himself, friends gone, reputation gone, will power almost gone, to find himself poor, hungry, feeding swine, he was suffering from the consequence of *answered* prayer. So Lot wanted Sodom and got it; Ahab craved Naboth's vineyard and seized it; Judas desired the thirty pieces and obtained them. 'They have received their reward in full' (Matthew 6:2). The Bible is full of answered prayers that ruined men. Again and again in history we see the old truth come true: 'He gave them what they asked for, but sent a wasting disease

167

upon them' (Psalm 106:15).

H. E. Fosdick[123]

No

The man who had been demon-possessed begged to go with him. Jesus did not let him, but said, 'Go home to your family and tell them how much the Lord has done for you, and how he has had mercy on you.'

Mark 5:18, 19

Are all the sincere, earnest, believing prayers of good people granted? The answer of experience is, 'No.' I have seen a distracted mother cling to the corpse of her child, refusing to believe that it was dead. She had prayed. God had promised. She had believed. He heard, he always heard. How could her child die? When at last the truth has forced itself upon her protesting mind, the distress deepens at the thought that God has not heard. There are many such days of desperate faith. Is God angry, as in the case of David (2 Samuel 12: 13–23), even where there is no such cause? Can it be that he is indifferent? Does he not know or has he forgotten? Is it any use to pray?

It was with such thoughts as these that I turned to my Bible and found the stories of three people whose requests were denied: Moses, when he prayed that he might go over into Canaan (Deuteronomy 3:23–29); Elijah, when he prayed that he might die (1 Kings 19:4); Paul, when he prayed for the removal of his affliction (2 Corinthians 12:8, 9).

Moses prayed that he might be allowed to complete his work. He had undertaken it at God's command. For forty years he had nursed and led an ungrateful people through the desert. The promised land was in sight. What more natural than that he should want to see his life-work completed? Besides, he would surely be needed in Canaan even more than in the desert. There were enemies to be driven out and the people to be settled. If he should leave them now, the work of forty years might fall to pieces. But, in spite of his record and his pleading, he dies with his work unfinished.

How often such things happen: the prayers of good men seem to fail; death calls, and the work of years is left unfinished, taking the parent and counsellor when he can least be spared, passing by the 'weak' and taking the 'strong'.

Elijah was mighty in prayer. God answered all his prayers except when, under a broom tree, suffering from mental and physical reaction, he prayed that he might die. What a mercy God does not always take us at our word!

Samuel Chadwick

No—because it wouldn't be good for you

'No,' is as truly an answer as 'Yes.' Refusal may be the only answer that would be in keeping with love, wisdom and truth. A child may cry for a razor and adults for equally unsafe, unsuitable and unwise things. Many have lived to thank God that he withstood their agonising entreaties at one time or another.

God never refuses without reason. He knows the past, in which there may be reasons for his having to answer, 'No.' Forgiven sin may disable. Moses and David were both examples of this (Deuteronomy 32:49–52; 2 Samuel 12:14). There are vessels that break on the potter's wheel and though another may be made, the original is impossible. The Lord knows the future as well as the past. The immediate may jeopardise the future. The eagerness for a mess of pottage may involve the loss of an inheritance.

Samuel Chadwick

The fact is that my prayer life cannot be tied directly to the results I expect or demand. I have had many opportunities by now to see that the things I want God to do in response to my prayers can be unhealthy for me. I have begun to see that worship and intercession are far more the business of aligning myself with God's purposes than asking him to align with mine.

Many times I have gone to prayer with results in mind. I wanted to gain control over the people and events I was praying about by dictating to the Father my views on how things should come out. When I do this, I am looking at people or events through an earthly lens and not a heavenly one. I am praying as though I know better than God what is best for the outcome.

Gordon Macdonald[124]

No—because there's something better

Delays are not denials and it pays to wait God's time. Moses got into Canaan and Elijah went to heaven by a far more glorious way than the one they would have chosen. No inspired prayer of faith is ever refused. 'No,' is never God's last word. God may refuse the route because he knows better; he took Moses into Canaan by a better way and in better company. I have known other people who have had to go by way of heaven to find the answer to their prayers. He took Elijah to heaven by a much more wonderful way than that of the grave. Elijah wanted to die but God gave his tired servant sleep and rest and sent him away to the hills for a holiday. To Paul he said, 'My grace is sufficient for you' (2 Corinthians 12:9), and taught him to glory in affliction. Similarly, in the experiences which try our faith, God sends help to us; and it is often through the tears of a broken heart that the vision comes. In heaven we shall find that our prayers have been interpreted according to God's infinite wisdom and love.

Samuel Chadwick

'When they came to the border of Mysia, they tried to enter Bithynia, but the Spirit of Jesus would not allow them to' (Acts 16:7). The Spirit of Jesus often shuts doors in the long corridors or life. We pass along, trying one after another, but find that they are all locked, in order that we may enter the one that he has opened for us (Revelation 3:7, 8).

F. B. Meyer

Some prayers may be right in themselves but inappropriate and perhaps the only answer God can give us is the insight to stop asking.

In Gethsemane, Jesus says to Peter, 'Do you think I cannot call on my Father, and he will at once put at my disposal more than twelve legions of angels? But how then would the Scriptures be fulfilled . . .' (Matthew 26:53, 54)? The request for angels would not have been wrong but it was silenced by a higher purpose and a deeper insight.

171

In predicting his death, Jesus said, 'Now my heart is troubled, and what shall I say? "Father, save me from this hour"? No, it was for this very reason I came to this hour. Father glorify your name' (John 12:27, 28)! Again a suggested prayer is never offered because the whole purpose of Jesus' life made such a petition inappropriate.

Jesus, praying for his disciples said, 'My prayer is not that you take them out of the world but that you protect them from the evil one' (John 17:15). To request the disciples' removal from the world would not have been consistent with their own need of experience or with the world's need of their testimony or with God's purpose of world redemption.

The Father's name, kingdom and will are the first concerns of all who pray the Christian way. Much too often we say, 'Thy will be done,' in tones of regretful resignation, as though it's a matter of putting up with what can't be helped. But that is not the meaning of the prayer. In the Lord's Prayer, having called God Father and acknowledged his majesty, and knowing how completely he can be trusted, we go on to ask that, before everything else, what he plans will come to pass and whatever he wishes to withhold, he will withhold. We put our lives into hands that we know are surer, steadier and wiser than ours could ever be. But that must mean that God's answer to our prayers must sometimes, perhaps often, be a kindly 'No'. His 'No' is always wiser than a 'Yes' would be.

R. E. O. White[125]

No—because things are not right

Prayer will not penetrate Godward if I am acting presumptuously (Deuteronomy 1:45). It was not enough for Israel to agonise. God had told them not to go up and fight the Amorites but they went presumptuously.

Prayer will not penetrate Godward if I reject his kingship (1 Samuel 8:18). To insist on living free from God's claims on my life will quickly block off my prayer from the throne.

Prayer will not penetrate Godward if I purposely desist from helping the needy (Proverbs 21:13). Our sensitivity is centred in things relating to our own interests. Self-absorption has clogged our reception to outside calls for help.

Prayer will not penetrate Godward if I regard iniquity in my heart (Psalm 66:18).

R. Arthur Mathews[126]

There are prayers that are offered for show—hypocritical, ostentatious prayers made 'standing in the synagogues and on the street corners to be seen by men' (Matthew 6:5). Such prayer is wrong in motive. It has no real relation to God at all but is aimed at people. And it gets what it seeks—the opinion of the passer-by (not always a complimentary one!). But it will get no more: 'I tell you the truth, they have received their reward in full.' Here is unanswered prayer—we might almost say unanswerable prayer.

The second unanswerable prayer is wrong in attitude: 'babbling like pagans, for they think they will be heard because of their many words' (Matthew 6:7). The pagan gods and goddesses were inconstant, subject to moods, whims and fits of jealousy, so the repetition of right formulas, compliments and promises of gifts were seen as necessary means of persuading them to do as they were being asked. Utterly different is the trusting relationship of a child to a loving and all-wise Father.

Another prayer which cannot be granted is one that is offered in a wrong spirit, as when the disciples suggested they should pray down fire from heaven on a Samaritan village where Jesus had been turned away. 'But Jesus turned and rebuked them' (Luke 9:55). It is possible to pray in a spirit of envy, even of rebelliousness. It is possible to pray with the heart smarting under the sense that others have been blessed more than we. Sometimes we pray selfishly, asking for ourselves gifts and favours or the solution of tangled situations which could only be granted to us at the expense of another's loss, hardship or embarrassment. But God has a great family and he loves them all.

Another kind of prayer that cannot be answered is that which is offered on a wrong basis—like that of the Pharisee in the temple rehearsing his own virtues as the ground of his thanksgiving (Luke 18:9–14).

Then there are the prayers which are unanswerable because they come from a wrong foundation of life and character. Such were the prayers of the scribes and Pharisees who devoured 'widows' houses and for a show make lengthy prayers' (Matthew 23:14, footnote). With such praying even Jesus has no patience; its only answer must be judgment. A good conscience is the first requirement of successful prayer. We certainly cannot earn God's blessing by our virtue; but if we are out of fellowship with God through something unconfessed and uncorrected, we ask in vain—until we ask for forgiveness.

R. E. O. White[127]

The real reason for the delay or failure we experience in our prayer lives lies simply in the difference between God's viewpoint and ours. In our asking, either we have not reached the wisdom that asks best, or we have not reached the unselfishness that is willing to sacrifice the smaller personal desire for the larger thing that affects the lives of many.

S. D. Gordon

So much of our prayer is selfish. It is 'Gimme . . . Gimme . . . Gimme'. We are not much better than the little boy who told the vicar that he didn't pray every night because there were some nights when he didn't want anything.

So much of our praying is coldly dutiful. It is better than no prayer at all, of course. But prayer without love has no suction. It doesn't draw the blessing down. The sick are not healed—or sustained in their serenity. God is not truly adored. Our neighbours are not blessed.

W. E. Sangster[128]

6

The Effects of Prayer

(Prayer changes more than things)

A Deeper Knowledge of God

Here I am! I stand at the door and knock. If anyone hears my voice and opens the door, I will go in and eat with him and he with me.   Revelation 3:20

Let him who boasts boast about this: that he understands and knows me, that I am the Lord, who exercises kindness, justice and righteousness on the earth, for in these I delight.   Jeremiah 9:24

The end of prayer is that I come to know God himself.

Oswald Chambers

Someone with a boat-hook which he fixes to the shore, could think that he was moving the land

177

towards him, whereas, in fact, he is getting closer to the land. Similarly, when we pray, we may think that we are drawing God nearer to us, when in fact we are drawing nearer to him.

E. Bickersteth

If you love someone, you want to spend time with that person; you listen to what he says; you remember everything about him: his ideas, his attitudes and the way he expresses himself. You get to know him very well. If you were separated from each other for a while, you would recognise his voice on the telephone and the way he expressed himself in his letters. If his voice changed in some way, or if his letters began to express things not in keeping with his character, you would be on the alert immediately. You would know that something was wrong.

So it should be between ourselves and God. God longs to reveal himself to us and to make us one with himself. So we must be prepared to spend much time alone with him, listening to him and frequently meditating deeply on Scripture.

Take his precious word deeply into your heart, let it sink into every part of your being, allowing the Holy Spirit to quicken it to you, for instruction, edification, guidance, encouragement and inspiration, but most of all simply that you may know him.

Audrey Merwood[129]

On some mornings God will reward us by making us feel his presence and the glorious quietening, heartening, invigorating sense of his nearness. But on other mornings, for various reasons, we shall not feel any devotional emotion at all; but surely we must obediently give God our wills and minds when we cannot offer him our feelings, and be prepared to keep our appointments with him when he does not reward our obedience with feelings.

Leslie D. Weatherhead[130]

Power From God

We have this treasure in jars of clay to show that this all-surpassing power is from God and not from us.

2 Corinthians 4:7

I tell you the truth, anyone who has faith in me will do what I have been doing. He will do even greater things than these, because I am going to the Father. And I will do whatever you ask in my name, so that the Son may bring glory to the Father. You may ask me for anything in my name, and I will do it. **John 14:12–14**

After they prayed, the place where they were meeting was shaken. And they were all filled with the Holy Spirit and spoke the word of God boldly. **Acts 4:31**

Prayer is the means by which Almighty God has chosen to release power into the world through the church. It is meant to be the very life-blood of all our activity and endeavour, bringing down blessing from heaven. This is the means by which God heals, cleanses, transforms and renews, and without it the body of Christ on earth is rendered anaemic, weak and ineffective. The fact that he has chosen to work in this way is a humbling mystery to us all.

Audrey Merwood[131]

Prayer does not release some mere force of man or nature. Prayer releases the immeasurable power and wealth of Almighty God! God says, in effect, that if you will pray, he will work! He, with whom nothing is impossible, who spoke, and worlds without number came into being, pledges his most holy and immutable word that, if we will but seek his face in prayer, he will work, and bring to pass great and mighty things such as have never been entertained in the mind and thought of man.

It is when people bow the knee and call upon God that, in a sense, they become as mighty as the Almighty. Do not misunderstand me. I am not being irreverent. I am only saying what he says in his holy word.

F. J. Huegel

'What's the potential of nuclear energy?' The correct answer must be something like, 'It's tremendous, probably beyond the immediate grasp of the human mind, and it has yet to be fully realised.' The same kind of thing—only more so—must be said of prayer. Its potential is synonymous with the power of God and, like that power, it's beyond our minds to grasp that immensity. No Christian has yet exhausted its capabilities.

Derek Prime[132]

Our gospel belongs to the miraculous. It was projected on the miraculous plane. It cannot be maintained but by the supernatural. Take the supernatural out of Christianity and its life and power are gone and it degenerates into mere morality.

Prayer brings into the affairs of earth a supernatural element. Our gospel, when truly presented, is the power of God. Never did the church need more than now those who can raise up everywhere memorials of God's supernatural power, of answers to prayer, of promises fulfilled.

E. M. Bounds

The prayers of holy men appease God's wrath, drive away temptations, resist and overcome the devil, rescind the decrees of God. Prayer cures sickness and obtains pardon; it arrests the sun in its course and stays the wheels of the chariot of the moon; it stops the mouths of lions and reconciles our suffering and weak faculties with the violence of torment and persecution; it pleases God and supplies all our need.

Jeremy Taylor

Prayer opened the Red Sea. Prayer brought water from the rock and bread from heaven. Prayer made the sun stand still. Prayer brought fire from the sky on Elijah's sacrifice. Prayer overthrew the army of Sennacherib. Well might Mary Queen of Scots say, 'I fear John Knox's prayers more than an army of ten thousand men.' Prayer has healed the sick. Prayer has raised the dead. Prayer brings about conversions.

J. C. Ryle

It will take violent dedication to prayer to bring the power of God into our lives. This violent earnestness will be most evident in discipline. For power in prayer takes much time. For this reason we must set priorities for our time. Many things will crowd around us to keep us from spending the time necessary for developing power in prayer.

Paul Yonggi Cho[133]

The prayers of all saints are a perpetual force against all the powers of darkness. These prayers are a mighty energy in overcoming the world, the flesh and the devil and in shaping the destiny of God's movements to overcome evil and gain the victory over the devil and all his works.

E. M. Bounds

When we turn to prayer . . . we may have to rebuke the powers of darkness. We are not to speak with them as we may speak with God; there is no question of holding a conversation with them. We proclaim the victory of Christ and command that they yield in his name.

Ken Gardiner[134]

The only way the devil can be rendered powerless today is as the truth and reality of the Saviour's victory through his death on the cross is administered by the believer on earth operating in the name of the Lord Jesus Christ. The truth of this is shown in the testimony of the Lord himself when the seventy he had sent out returned to render an account of their ministry. Jesus said then, 'I saw Satan fall like lightning from heaven' (Luke 10:18).

If we are to grapple not with flesh-and-blood adversaries but with principalities and powers in the heavenlies, we need to come to grips with one basic truth of God's Word: that when God raised Jesus Christ from the dead and set him in the seat of authority far above all, he made us co-sharers with him in every stage of the mighty finished work and then seated us with him.

From only one position is it safe to approach and resist Satan, and that is from this position in Christ in the highest heavenlies. From this position Satan and his hosts are completely vulnerable.

R. Arthur Mathews[135]

God's People Changed

We ... are being transformed into his likeness with ever-increasing glory, which comes from the Lord who is the Spirit. 2 Corinthians 3:18

... an instrument for noble purposes, made holy, useful to the Master and prepared to do any good work. 2 Timothy 2:21

Pray also for me, that whenever I open my mouth, words may be given me so that I will fearlessly make known the mystery of the gospel. Ephesians 6:19

Put on the full armour of God so that you can take your stand against the devil's schemes. Ephesians 6:11

Do not be anxious about anything, but in everything, by prayer and petition, with thanksgiving, present your requests to God. And the peace of God, which transcends all understanding, will guard your hearts and minds in Christ Jesus. Philippians 4:6, 7

Transformed from within

Prayer is the appointed way of giving Jesus an opportunity to exercise his supernatural powers of salvation. And in so doing, he desires to make use of us. Through prayer we should give Jesus the opportunity of gaining access to our souls, our bodies, our homes, our neighbourhoods, our countries, the whole world, the fellowship of believers and the unsaved.

To pray is nothing more than to lie in the sunshine of his grace, to expose our distress of body and soul to those healing rays which can in a wonderful way counteract and render ineffective the bacteria of sin. To be a man or woman of prayer is to take this sun-cure, to give Jesus, with his wonder-working power, access to our distress night and day.

O. Hallesby[136]

We pray not in order that God may be *in*structed, but in order that we may be *con*structed.

Augustine

Prayer is God's creation and recreation of us into the likeness of Christ.

Lindsay Dewar

Prayer is the central avenue God uses to transform us. If we are unwilling to change, we will abandon prayer as a noticeable characteristic of our lives. The closer we come to the heartbeat of God, the more we see our need and the more we desire to be conformed to Christ.

Richard Foster[137]

Christian prayer is giving God an opportunity to do what he wants, what he has always been trying in vain, perhaps for years, to do in our lives, hindered by our unreadiness, our lack of receptivity, our closed hearts and unresponsive minds. God stands over our lives like the Master over Jerusalem, saying, 'How often I have longed . . . but you were not willing' (Matthew 23:37).

H. E. Fosdick[138]

When I pray, I open the doors of my life to God and let him in. And he comes in. He comes in to purify and to transform my life. He cleans the place up a bit, moving the furniture around and throwing some of it out. He cleans the windows, so I can see other people and the world outside more clearly. He stocks the fridge and the deep-freeze with food to keep me going. He takes my temperature, puts me to bed and prescribes medicines to make me better. He ticks me off and cheers me up according to my need. That, of course, is picture language. But I hope you see what I mean. The presence of God judges, purifies, feeds, heals and strengthens me.

Evan Pilkington[139]

Prayer over everything can quiet every distraction, hush every anxiety and lift every care from care-enslaved lives and care-bewildered hearts. Only prayer in everything can drive dull care away, relieve of unnecessary heart burdens and save from the besetting sin of worrying over things which we cannot help. Only prayer can bring into the heart and mind 'the peace of God which transcends all understanding' and keep mind and heart free from carking care.

E. M. Bounds

Prayer opens our lives to the guidance of God because, by its very nature, it encourages the receptive mood. The dominant mood today is active; but some things never come into life until a person is receptive. That a boy should run many errands for his father, and should be faithful and energetic in doing it, is of great importance; but the most far-reaching consequences in that boy's life are likely to come from some quiet hour when he sits with his father and has his eyes opened to a new idea of life, which his father never could give him in his more active moods.

H. E. Fosdick[140]

Some of God's people never seem able to get on from the time of their conversion; they remain babies all their lives. Others always seem to be advancing; they press on, adding grace to grace, faith to faith and strength to strength. You feel warmed by their company.

Why is it that some believers are so much brighter and holier than others? I believe the difference mostly arises from differences in their prayer lives.

J. C. Ryle

It is in prayer that our motives are tested; that we wait for the Spirit to show us whether we are asking the right thing in the right way. It is in prayer that we become conscious of our need of faith; that Jesus teaches and inspires faith; that we prove the reality of our faith by our perseverence.

Andrew Murray

'Jacob was left alone, and a man wrestled with him till daybreak' (Genesis 32:24). The story of the angel wrestling with Jacob (Genesis 32:22–32) is an instance of God's earnest desire to take from us all that hinders our best and highest life, while we re-sist with might and main. There was much evil in Jacob that needed to be laid aside and so the love of God came close to him in the form of an angel to wrestle with him. At first he held his own; but what-ever it is that is making someone whom God wants to bless stand out against him, God will touch. It may be as natural or small as a hip socket, but if it robs us of spiritual blessing, God will touch it, and because of its evil influence, he will take notice of it and cause our schemes to go wrong and our strength to dry up.

Then Jacob stopped defending and resisting and clung to his opponent. It is good when we come to this attitude, for there is nothing God will not do for the soul that clings to him in absolute weakness.

Three things happened. His name was changed, indicating a changed character. Israel means prince with God. The cheat, the weak character, became royal, and there is only one road to such royalty: that of self-surrender and faith. He was given power, and those who would have such power and authority must first yield to God. He saw God, and our moments of vision will also come after nights of wrestling.

F. B. Meyer

As we go on in the work of prayer, there is a deep-ening of spiritual quality, an intensification of love, and with love all the other virtues flowering every moment into new and richer things.

Shirley C. Hughson[141]

Jesus can make happy those who trust him and call on him, whatever their condition. He can give them peace of heart in a prison, contentment in the midst of poverty, comfort in the midst of bereavements, joy on the brink of death.

Prayer can lighten our burdens however heavy. It can bring to our side one who will help to bear them. Prayer can open a door for us when our way seems hedged up. It can bring one who will say, 'This is the way; walk in it' (Isaiah 30:21). Prayer can let in a ray of hope when all our earthly prospects seem dark. It can bring the one who can fill our hearts with himself and say to the waves inside us, 'Quiet! Be still' (Mark 4:39).

J. C. Ryle

[Prayer] is something like building a house with a completely reliable architect. He draws up the plan, a much better plan than we could draw. All the time we make suggestions and tell him what we like and think good. Some of them are impossible and would wreck the plan; others he incorporates into the scheme – so skilfully sometimes that we do not at first recognise them. But we are content to leave the whole thing in his hands, knowing that in the end all will be well. And each day we eagerly watch its progress.

H. Northcott[142]

Prayer alters people on the inside, alters their minds and attitudes to things. The point of praying is not that we get things from God but that we learn by prayer to detect the difference between God's order and God's permissive will. God's order is— no pain, no sickness, no devil, no sin; his permissive will is all these things—the 'soup' we are in just now. What a person needs to do is to get hold of

God's order in the kingdom on the inside, and then he will begin to see how to handle the riddle of the universe on the outside.

Oswald Chambers

Equipped for work

It is the privilege of every child of God to have the power of God in his service. Sometimes you will hear people stand up in a meeting and say, 'I am trying to serve God in my poor, weak way.' Well, if you are trying to serve God in your poor, weak way, quit it; your duty is to serve God in his strong, triumphant way.

But you say, 'I have no natural ability.' Then get a supernatural ability. The religion of Jesus is a supernatural religion from start to finish, and we should live our lives in supernatural power, the power of God through Jesus Christ, and we should perform our service with supernatural power, the power of God ministered by the Holy Spirit through Jesus Christ.

You say, 'I have no natural gifts.' Then get supernatural gifts. The Holy Spirit is promised to every believer that he may obtain the supernatural gifts which qualify him for the particular service to which God calls him.

R. A. Torrey

Praying gives sense, brings wisdom, broadens and strengthens the mind. Thought is not only brightened and clarified in prayer, but thought is born in prayer. We can learn more in an hour praying than from many hours in studying.

Prayer unites the soul to God. God looks at us in love and would have us share in his good work. So he moves us to pray for what it is he wants to do.

Julian of Norwich

Prayer should result in an enlarged outreach through loving concern—a sense of mission, of sharing God's love and kindness in practical ways.

R. Rinker[143]

The praying Christian is the strong, thriving Christian, 'strong in the Lord and in his mighty power' (Ephesians 6:10). Ivy, which unsupported would remain on the ground, by clinging to some neighbouring tree or building, can rise high into the air; the more the wind blows, the more it clings to its support, and so is kept safe. Similarly, the Christian, though naturally weak, is linked by prayer to God; the more dangers and difficulties there are, the more closely he clings to God and so is strengthened by him.

E. Bickersteth

The Christian soul is a sailing boat . . . The technique of the spiritual life teaches us how to use the sails of prayer and discipline and to catch the wind of God to waft us on our course to heaven. Our Lord himself compares the Holy Spirit to the wind . . . We start in a land-locked bay; there seems scarcely any breeze and we row hard to get the boat moving. As it moves out of the bay, it enters the wide seas; the wind fills the sails and sweeps the boat along.

H. Northcott[144]

We must understand that prayer is of itself a divinely appointed and effective *work*, and it is a great mistake for those who 'do' to think that everyone else should be 'doing' something too. Indeed, very often it is only because of the faithful, secret work of the pray-ers that the do-ers are enabled to be effective anyway. Paul often asked his fellow-Christians to *pray* for him in order that he might *do* his job more effectively.

Audrey Merwood[145]

Work without prayer produces clever ineffectiveness. Prayer without work has not been wholly sterile of spiritual gain but it is not a maximum for God. In work and prayer together the blessing of the Lord rests most richly.

W. E. Sangster [146]

Prayer reaches to everything that concerns a person, whether it be his body, his mind or his soul. Prayer takes in the wants of the body—food, clothes, business, finance, in fact, everything which belongs to this life as well as those things which have to do with eternal interests. Its achievements are seen not only in the large things of earth but more especially in what might be called the little things of life.

E. M. Bounds

When we pray for help in trouble or for healing in sickness or for deliverance in persecution, God may not give us what we ask for, for that may not be his wise and loving will for us. But he will answer our prayer in his own way. He will not let us down in our hour of need. He will give us the patience, courage and strength to endure our suffering, the ability to rise above it and the assurance of his presence in all that we are called to pass through.

Billy Graham[147]

God's Will Done

You will be done on earth as it is in heaven.
Matthew 6:10

May the God of peace ... equip you with everything good for doing his will, and may he work in us what is pleasing to him, through Jesus Christ, to whom be glory for ever and ever. **Hebrews 13:20, 21**

Our God has a great heart which yearns over his poor runaway world and each person in it. He longs to have the effects of sin removed and the original image restored. He takes the initiative. Yet everything that is done for people must be through their willingness. The obstacles are many and stubborn. There is a keen, cunning pretender-prince who is a past-master at handling people. There are warped wills, blurred consciences, dulled minds. Sin has stained people's lives, warped their judgment, sapped their wills and blurred their vision.

But God says, 'Call to me and I will answer you and tell you great and unsearchable things you do not know' (Jeremiah 33:3). If someone calls, he has already turned his face towards God and aligned his purpose with God's. Beset by difficulties, he longs for freedom; God saw his difficulties long before and longed to remove them; now that he and the person have come to an agreement, he can do so. Through the willing will of the person, God eagerly works out his purpose.

Does prayer influence God? The answer is, 'Yes

and no.' It does not influence his purpose but it
does influence the action. Every right thing that
has ever been prayed for, God has already pur-
posed to do. But he is hindered in his purposes by
our lack of willingness. When we learn his purposes and make them our prayers, we are giving
him the opportunity to act. It is a double opportunity: it checkmates Satan's opposition; it opens
the path to God and rids it of the obstacles.

S. D. Gordon

Someone once asked me whether there was any
danger of our thinking that our prayers moved
God to love and to be willing to bless people. At
the time, we were just passing some water pipes
which were carrying water from a mountain stream
to a town some distance away.

'Look at the pipes,' was my answer. They did not
make the water willing to flow down from the
mountain, nor did they give the water its power to
refresh: that was its very nature. All they could do
was decide the direction of the flow. By laying the
pipes, the people of the town were saying, in effect,
'We want refreshment here.' Similarly, it is God's
nature to love and to bless and he longs to do so.
But he has left it to prayer to decide where the
blessing is to come. He has committed it to his believing people to bring the living water to the
desert places. The will of God to bless is dependent
on the will of God's people to say where the blessing must come.

Andrew Murray

There are people who put prayer first and arrange
everything else around it. These are the people

who are doing the most for God in winning people to Christ, in solving problems, in awakening churches, in supplying people and money for God's work, in supporting those in the thick of the battle, in keeping the old earth sweet a little longer.

They are part of a very secret service. We probably pass some of these people by without a second glance; ordinary, insignificant-looking people, perhaps; but people who truly pray as the Spirit of God guides and inspires and are, therefore, doing far more for the church, the world and for God than a hundred others who receive more attention.

S. D. Gordon

We have two fundamentally opposed ideas of prayer: one, that by begging we may change the will of God and curry favour or win gifts by coaxing; the other, that prayer is offering God the opportunity to say to us, give to us and do through us what he wills. Only the second is Christian.

Prayer really does things. It cannot change God's intention but it does change God's action. When Isaiah said, 'Here am I, send me,' he did not alter in the least the divine purpose but he did release it. God could do then what before he could not.

God had long intended that Africa should be evangelised. When Livingstone cried, 'O God, help me to paint this dark continent white,' he did not alter God's intention but he did alter God's action. Power broke loose that before had been pent up; the co-operation of a man's prayer, backed by his life, opened a way for the divine purpose.

In prayer you align yourselves to the purpose and power of God and he is able to do things through you that he couldn't do otherwise. For this is an open universe, where some things are left open, contingent upon our doing them. For God left certain things open to prayer—things which will never be done except as we pray.

E. Stanley Jones

God's Promises Proved

Call upon me in the day of trouble; I will deliver you and you will honour me. **Psalm 50:15**

No matter how many promises God has made, they are 'Yes' in Christ. And so through him the 'Amen' is spoken by us to the glory of God. **2 Corinthians 1:20**

Prayer is asking, seeking and knocking at a door for something we have not which we want and which God has promised to us.

E. M. Bounds

Every promise of Scripture is a writing of God which may be pleaded before him with this reasonable request, 'Do as you have said.' The Creator will not cheat the creature who depends on his truth; and, far more, the heavenly Father will not break his word to his own child.

C. H. Spurgeon

Prayer opens an outlet for the promises, removes hindrances, puts them into working order and then into effect. More than this, prayer, like faith, obtains promises and increases their effectiveness. God's promises were to Abraham and his descendants but many obstacles stood in the way of their fulfilment. Prayer removed all these and made a highway for the promises to be more quickly and completely fulfilled.

Prayer is a spiritual energy which makes way for and brings into practical realisation the promises of God. God's promises cover all things which relate to life and godliness, body and soul, time and eternity. Prayer holds these promises in keeping and in fruition. Promises are God's golden fruit to be plucked by the hand of prayer. Promises are God's seed to be sown and tilled by prayer.

Promises are like rain falling in full showers and prayer, like the pipes which transmit, preserve and direct the rain, makes these promises become local and personal, so that they can bless, refresh and fertilise. Prayer takes hold of the promises, removes obstacles and makes a highway for their glorious fulfilment.

E. M. Bounds

When reading Scripture, we should be alert to discover what God has promised to do, and then we should lay hold of his promises.

We shall discover promises for adversity and prosperity; promises of peace, guidance, protection, strength, deliverance, joy, and a hundred other blessings.

We can adopt three attitudes to God's promises. We can come short of them by devaluing them to the level of past experience. It is possible for us to so tone them down that we come far short of what God is offering us. We can stagger and waver in unbelief because the risk involved seems too great or because the promise seems too good to be true. We can be fully assured and receive the promises.

With God, promise and performance are inseparable. 'No matter how many promises God has made, they are "Yes" in Christ. And so through him the "Amen" is spoken by us to the glory of God' (2 Corinthians 1:20).

When God makes a promise, that promise is his 'Yes' and Jesus is the guarantee of its fulfilment. The 'Yes' is God's. 'Amen' is my response of faith—my expression, of confidence that the promise will be fulfilled. I say 'Amen' in this sense when I cash a cheque signed by another person.

It is a poor compliment if we respond to God's gracious 'Yes' with a faltering 'Amen'.

J. Oswald Sanders[148]

God's Work Revived

'Bring the whole tithe into the storehouse, that there may be food in my house. Test me in this,' says the Lord Almighty, 'and see if I will not throw open the floodgates of heaven and pour out so much blessing that you will not have room enough for it.'

Malachi 3:10

Will you not revive us again, that your people may rejoice in you? **Psalm 85:6**

Lord, I have heard of your fame; I stand in awe of your deeds, O Lord. Renew them in our day, in our time make them known; in wrath remember mercy.

Habakkuk 3:2

Usually when God intends greatly to bless a church, it will begin in this way: two or three persons in it are distressed at the low state of affairs and become troubled even to anguish.

Perhaps they do not know of their common grief

but they begin to pray with flaming desire and un-tiring importunity. The passion to see the church revived rules them. They think of it as they go to rest. They dream of it on their bed. They muse on it in the streets. This one things consumes them. They suffer great heaviness and continual sorrow in heart for perishing sinners. They travail in birth for souls.

C. H. Spurgeon

Every true revival has had its earthly origins in prayer. Prayer could work as marvellous results to-day as it ever could if the church would only betake itself to praying, real praying, prevailing praying. There seem to be increasing signs that the church is awakening to that fact. Here and there God is laying on individual ministers and churches a burden of prayer that they have never known be-fore. Many are getting entirely disgusted with mere machinery and with man-made revivals and are learning to depend on God. Ministers are crying to God day and night for power. In a few places, per-haps many, churches or portions of churches are meeting together in the early morning hours and late evening hours crying to God for abundant rain. There are indications of the coming of a mighty and widespread revival.

What is needed is a general revival but if we can-not have a general revival sweeping over the whole earth, we can have local revivals and state revivals and national revivals. It is not necessary that the whole church get to praying to begin with. Great revivals always begin first in the hearts of a few men and women whom God arouses by his Spirit to believe in him as a living God, as a God who answers prayer, and on whose hearts he lays a burden from which no rest can be found except in importunate crying to God. May he, by his Spirit, lay such a burden on hearts today. I believe he will.

R. A. Torrey

I believe that just as some churches have had a foretaste of God's blessing as they have come before him in prayer, whether in triplets or in any other group, the church . . . as a whole will experience the outpouring of God's Spirit—as and when it is prepared to seek God, and call on him, and plead with him, and implore him, and wait on him, and serve him in truth with all its heart.

All the time we squabble among ourselves about our doctrinal differences, denominational distinctives, church government and order, scriptural interpretation, evangelistic methodology, social action or anything else, we will postpone or even forfeit the possibility of an outpouring of God's Spirit.

What we need from now on is not more programmes for evangelism so much as more prayer for an awakening. Evangelism will surely occur in the wake of an awakening, but an awakening will not occur as a result of more evangelism. You can have evangelism without revival, but you can't have revival without evangelism. Evangelism helps to sustain revival, not to start it. Prayer helps to start a revival and sustain it. A growing church prays and a praying church grows.

Brian Mills[149]

Prayer in the Bible

Some Bible Teaching on Prayer

2 Chronicles 7:14; Psalm 34:6, 15; 37:1–7; 50:23; 62:8; 66:16–20; 100:1–4; Isaiah 43:21; 65:24; Matthew 6:6–15; 7:7–11; 18:19, 20; 26:36–44; Mark 9:28, 29; Luke 11:1–13; 18:1–14; John 15:7; 16:23, 24; Romans 8:26, 27; 2 Corinthians 1:11; 12:8, 9; Ephesians 3:20, 21; 5:19, 20; 6:16, 19; Philippians 4:4–7; 1 Thessalonians 5:16–18; 1 Timothy 2:1, 2; Hebrews 4:16; 11; 13:15; James 1:5–7; 4:2, 3; 5:13–18; 1 John 3:21–24; 5:14–17; Revelation 3:20

Some Bible Prayers

Longing for God: Psalm 42; 63
Praise worship, thanksgiving: Exodus 15:1–18; Deuteronomy 32:1–43; Judges 5; 2 Samuel 22; 1 Chronicles 16:7–36; Psalm 8; 18; 65; 105; 136; 145; Isaiah 38:9–20;

Daniel 2:20–23; Luke 1:46–55, 68–79; Romans 16: 25–27; 2 Corinthians 1:3, 4; Ephesians 1:3–10; 3:20, 21; Philippians 4:20; 1 Thessalonians 3:11–13; Hebrews 13: 20, 21; 1 Peter 5:10, 11; Jude 24, 25; Revelation 5:9–4

For the honour and glory of God: 1 Kings 18:36, 37; 2 Kings 19:14–19; Psalm 74: 10, 11, 18–23; Matthew 6:9–13; Luke 11:2–4; John 12:27, 28

To see God's glory: Exodus 33:18–23

For wisdom and guidance: 1 Kings 3:6–14; 2 Chronicles 1:7–12; Psalm 25

For blessing: Genesis 32:22–32; Exodus 33:12–17; 2 Samuel 7:18–29

For a sign: Judges 6:11–40

For God's people: John 17:6–26; Ephesians 1:16–23; 3: 14–19; Philippians 1:3–11; Colossians 1:3–14; 1 Thessalonians 1:2, 3; 2:13; 3:9–13; 5:23; 2 Thessalonians 1:3; 2:13, 16, 17; 3:16; 2 Timothy 1:3, 4; Philemon 4–6

For help in trouble: Genesis 32:9–12; 2 Kings 19:14–19; Isaiah 37:14–20; Psalm 40; 86; 102; 140; 143; Acts 4: 24–30

In desperation: 1 Samuel 1:1–18; Job 10; 13; 14; Psalm 22; 69; 88; Jonah 2; Matthew 26:36–44; 27:46; Mark 14:32–39; 15:34; Luke 22:39–46

In bewilderment: Psalm 10; Jeremiah 12; Habakkuk 1

Responding to God's giving: 1 Chronicles 29:10–20

For a town or nation: Genesis 18:22–33; Exodus 32: 11–14; Deuteronomy 9:25–29; 1 Samuel 7:7–9; Nehemiah 1:4–11

For vindication: Job 27–31; Psalm 26; 35; 43

Confession of sin and desire for forgiveness: Exodus 32: 31–35; Ezra 9; Nehemiah 9; Job 42:1–6; Psalm 51; 130; Daniel 9:4–19; Luke 18:13

For enemies: Luke 23:34; Acts 7:59, 60

Some Names or Attributes of God

Genesis 14:18; 17:1; 18:25; 22:14; Exodus 3:14; 6:3; 15:2, 3, 26; 34:6, 7; Numbers 23:19; Joshua 24:2; 1 Samuel 7:12; Nehemiah 2:4; Job 6:10; Psalm 23:1; 27:1; 34:8; 43:4; 46:1; 62:7; 80:7, 14; Song of Songs 2:4; Isaiah 1:4; 40:28; 53:11; Jeremiah 10:7, 10; 16:19; 19:15; 23:6; 32:17, 18, 27; Malachi 2:10; 3:6; Mark 10:18; John 3:16; 4:24; 1 Timothy 1:17; 2:3, 4; 6:15; James 1:17; 1 John 1:5, 9; 4:8

SOURCES

Details of numbered sources in the text (some books referred to are out of print):

1 *Effective Prayer*, R.C. Sproul, Scripture Union, 1986, p. 56

2 *Breaking the Prayer Barrier*, M. Baughen, Shaw, 1961, p. 78

3 *Touch the World through Prayer*, W. E. Duewel, Marshall Pickering, 1986, p. 143

4 *Standing in the Gap*, K. Gardiner, Kingsway, 1985, pp. 119, 120

5 *Ordering Your Private World*, G. Macdonald, Highland Books, 1985, p. 163

6 *Imagination*, C. Forbes, MARC Europe, 1986, pp. 170, 171, 173

7 *Standing in the Gap*, K. Gardiner, Kingsway, 1985, p. 118

8 *Moving Prayer*, R. Budd, MARC Europe, 1987, pp. 134, 135

9 K. N. Taylor, *Essays on Prayer*, A. W. Tozer & others, IVP, 1973, pp. 40, 41

10 *The Hour That Changes the World*, D. Eastman, Baker Book House, 1978, p. 99

11 *What Happens When God Answers Prayer*, E. Christenson, Word, 1986, p. 176

12 *People in Prayer*, J. White, IVP, 1977, p. 52

13 *The Hour That Changes the World*, D. Eastman, Baker Book House, 1978, pp. 42, 47–49

14 *Ordering Your Private World*, G. Macdonald, Highland Books, 1985, pp. 164, 165

15 *Celebration of Discipline*, R. Foster, Hodder & Stoughton, 1980, pp. 132, 133

16 *The Christian Response*, M. Quoist, Gill, 1965, p. 64

17 *The Christian Response*, M. Quoist, Gill, 1965, pp. 62–65

18 *Discipleship*, D. Watson, Hodder & Stoughton, 1981, pp. 123, 124

19 *The Suffering God*, C. Ohlrich, SPCK, 1983, pp. 98,

SOURCES

99

20 *The Suffering God*, C. Ohlrich, SPCK, 1983, pp. 112, 113

21 *God of Surprises*, G. W. Hughes, Darton Longman Todd, 1985, pp. 85, 86

22 *Man, God & Prayer*, H. Northcott, SPCK, 1954, p. 106

23 *The Fight*, J. White, IVP, 1977, p. 27

24 *Teach Us to Pray*, D. A. Hubbard, IVP, 1983, p. 35

25 *Your Confirmation*, J. R. W. Stott, Hodder & Stoughton 1958, p. 93

26 *Prayers That Live*, F. Colquhoun, SPCK, 1981, p. 43

27 *Ashburnham Insights: Intercession*, T. Pain, Kingsway, 1986, p. 22

28 *Encountering Light*, G. ffrench-Beytagh, Collins, 1978, p. 43

29 *Prayers That Live*, F. Colquhoun, SPCK, 1981, pp. 9, 10

30 *Come into His Presence*, J. Wallis, Kingsway, 1987, pp. 119, 120

31 *Practical Prayer*, D. Prime, Hodder & Stoughton, 1985, p. 92

32 *Power in Preaching*, W. E. Sangster, Epworth, 1958, pp. 28, 29

33 *The Dynamics of Spiritual Life*, R. F. Lovelace, Paternoster, 1979, pp. 393, 394

34 *Keys to Effective Prayer*, G. Strong, Marshalls, 1985, p. 87

35 *Standing in the Gap*, K. Gardiner, Kingsway, 1985, pp. 94, 96

36 *Listening to God*, J. Huggett, Hodder & Stoughton, 1986, pp. 56, 57

37 Veronica Zundel, *Alive to God*, Jan/Mar, 1988, Scripture Union, p. 69

38 *Celebration of Discipline*, R. Foster, Hodder & Stoughton, 1978, p. 15

39 *Knowing God*, J. I. Packer, Hodder & Stoughton, 1973, pp. 18, 19

SOURCES

40 *Celebration of Discipline*, R. Foster, Hodder & Stoughton, IVP, 1978, p. 26

41 K. N. Taylor, *Essays on Prayer*, A. W. Tozer & others, IVP, 1973, p. 41

42 *Prayers That Live*, F. Colquhoun, SPCK, 1981, p. 4

43 *Contemplative Prayer*, S. C. Hughson, 1935, SPCK, pp. 107, 159

44 *Heaven in Ordinary*, A. Ashwin, Mayhew McCrimmon, 1985, pp. 27, 28

45 *Prayer*, O. Hallesby, IVF, 1948, p. 114

46 *Teach Us to Pray*, W. E. Sangster, Epworth, 1951, p. 24

47 *Encountering the Depths*, Mother Mary Clare, Darton Longman Todd, 1981, p. 32

48 *Listening to God*, J. Huggett, Hodder & Stoughton, 1986, p. 53

49 *Through the Year with David Watson*, ed. J. Watson, Hodder & Stoughton, 1982, p. 293

50 *The Business of Heaven*, C. S. Lewis, Collins, p. 76

51 *Jesus—Man of Prayer*, Sister Margaret Magdalen, Hodder & Stoughton, 1987, pp. 33, 34

52 *The Meaning of Prayer*, H. E. Fosdick, Collins, 1915, p.18

53 J. I. Packer, *My Path of Prayer*, ed. D. Hanes, Walter, 1981, p. 58

54 *Effective Prayer*, J. O. Sanders, CIM, 1961, p. 67

55 *Ashburnham Insights: Intercession*, T. Pain, Kingsway, 1986, p. 50

56 *Prayer Power Unlimited*, J. O. Sanders, Highland Books, 1977, p. 147

57 *Praying through Paradox*, C. Elliott, Collins, 1987, pp. 48, 50

58 *God of Surprises*, G. W. Hughes, Darton Longman Todd, 1985, p. 99

59 *Learning to Pray*, E. Pilkington, Darton Longman Todd, 1986, pp. 44–46

60 *Restoring Your Spiritual Passion*, G. Macdonald, Highland Books, 1986, pp. 151, 152

SOURCES

61 *School for Prayer*, Archbishop A. Bloom, Darton Longman Todd, 1970, pp. 67–70

62 *How to Grow*, K. N. Taylor, Highland Books, 1985, pp. 59, 60

63 *The Pattern of Prayer*, W. E. Sangster, Epworth, p. 78

64 *School for Prayer*, Archbishop A. Bloom, Darton Longman Todd, 1970, p. 7

65 *Prayer*, O. Hallesby, IVF, 1948, pp. 85, 86

66 *Contemplative Prayer*, S. C. Hughson, SPCK, 1935, pp. 165, 167, 168

67 *The Strong and the Weak*, P. Tournier, Highland, 1984, pp. 250, 251

68 *Encountering the Depths*, Mother Mary Clare, Darton Longman Todd, 1981, p. 8

69 *The Meaning of Prayer*, H. E. Fosdick, Collins, 1915, pp. 54, 59, 60

70 *Encountering Light*, G. ffrench-Beytagh, Collins, 1975, p. 36

71 *The Meaning of Prayer*, H. E. Fosdick, Collins, 1915, p. 102

72 *The Meaning of Prayer*, H. E. Fosdick, Collins, 1915, p. 18

73 *The Meaning of Prayer*, H. E. Fosdick, SCM, 1921, pp. 23, 24

74 *People in Prayer*, J. White, IVP, 1977, p. 15

75 *Till Armageddon*, B. Graham, Hodder & Stoughton, 1981, p. 155

76 *You Can Make a Difference*, T. Campolo, Word, 1985, pp. 114, 115

77 *Encountering Light*, G. ffrench-Beytagh, Collins, 1975, p. 35

78 *Jesus—Man of Prayer*, Sister Margaret Magdalen, Hodder & Stoughton, 1987, p. 72

79 *The Way of an Intercessor*, A Merwood, Kingsway, 1985, p. 74

80 *The Practice of Prayer*, G. Campbell Morgan, Hodder & Stoughton, p.8.

81 *Christian Counter-Culture*, J. R. W. Stott, IVP, 1978,

p. 151

82 *Breaking the Prayer Barrier*, M. Baughen, Shaw, 1961, pp. 36, 45

83 *Standing in the Gap*, K. Gardiner, Kingsway, 1985, p. 95

84 *Teach Us to Pray*, D. A. Hubbard, IVP, 1983, pp. 42–47

85 *Prayer Power Unlimited*, J. O. Sanders, Highland Books, 1977, p. 64

86 *The Practice of Prayer*, G. Campbell Morgan, Hodder & Stoughton, p. 120

87 *Prayer Power Unlimited*, J. O. Sanders, Highland Books, 1977, p. 80

88 *Prayer for All Times*, P. Charles, Collins, 1983, pp. 75, 76

89 *Keys to Effective Prayer*, G. Strong, Marshalls, 1985, p. 47

90 *Teach Us to Pray*, W. E. Sangster, Epworth, 1951, pp. 15, 16

91 *Breaking the Prayer Barrier,* M. Baughen, Shaw, 1981, pp. 104, 105

92 *Prayers of the New Testament*, D. Coggan, Hodder & Stoughton, 1967, pp. 16, 17

93 *Prayer Secrets,* Guy H. King, Marshall, Morgan & Scott, pp. 75–77

94 J. O. Fraser, *Mountain Rain*, E. Crossman, OMF, 1982, pp. 65, 66

95 *Choice Sayings*, Hudson Taylor, OMF

96 *Choice Sayings,* Hudson Taylor, OMF

97 *Effective Prayer*, J. O. Sanders, CIM, 1961, p. 9

98 *The Meaning of Prayer*, H. E. Fosdick, Collins, 1915, p. 130

99 *Effective Prayer*, J. O. Sanders, CIM, 1961, p. 18

100 *Prayer*, O. Hallesby, IVF, 1948, p. 22

101 *Prayer*, O. Hallesby, IVF, 1948, p. 21

102 *Adventures in Prayer*, C. Marshall. Hodder & Stoughton, 1975, pp. 34, 35

103 *Effective Prayer*, J. O. Sanders, CIM, 1961, pp. 14, 24

104 *Effective Prayer*, R. C. Sproul, Scripture Union, 1986, p. 57

105 *People in Prayer*, J. White, IVP, 1977, pp. 121, 122

106 James Jones, *Alive to God*, October–December 1987, Scripture Union

107 *Through the Year with David Watson*, ed. J. Watson, Hodder & Stoughton, 1982, p. 297

108 *The Meaning of Prayer*, H. E. Fosdick, Collins, 1915, p. 152

109 James Graham, *Daily Bread*, January 1981, Scripture Union

110 *I Want to be a Christian*, J. I. Packer, Kingsway, 1985

111 *Teach Us to Pray*, W. E. Sangster, Epworth, pp. 25, 26

112 *The Pattern of Prayer*, W. E. Sangster, Epworth, pp. 22, 23

113 *Why Jesus Never Wrote a Book*, W. E. Sangster, Epworth, p. 75

114 Leith Samuel, *Essays on Prayer*, A. W. Tozer & others, IVP, 1973, pp. 74, 75

115 Raymond Ortlund, *Essays on Prayer*, A. W. Tozer & others, IVP, 1973, p. 35

116 *They Teach Us to Pray*, R. E. O. White, Arthur James, London 1967, p. 189

117 *Essays on Prayer*, A. W. Tozer & others, IVP, 1973, p. 70

118 *They Teach Us to Pray*, R. E. O. White, Arthur James, London 1967, pp. 185–188

119 *Breaking the Prayer Barrier*, M. Baughen, Shaw, 1981, p. 32

120 *The Meaning of Prayer*, H. E. Fosdick, Collins, 1915, p. 151

121 *Effective Prayer*, R. C. Sproul, Scripture Union, 1984, pp. 83, 84

122 *A Step Further*, J. Eareckson & S. Estes, Pickering & Inglis, 1978, p. 157

123 *The Meaning of Prayer*, H. E. Fosdick, Collins, 1915, p. 172

SOURCES

124 *Ordering Your Private World*, G. Macdonald, Highland Books, 1985, p. 160

125 *They Teach Us to Pray*, R. E. O. White, Arthur James, London 1967, pp. 183–185

126 *Born for Battle*, R. A. Mathews, OMF, 1978, pp. 99, 100

127 *They Teach Us to Pray*, R. E. O. White, Arthur James, London 1967, pp. 180–183

128 *The Pattern of Prayer*, W. E. Sangster, Epworth, p. 79

129 *The Way of an Intercessor*, A. Merwood, Kingsway, 1985, pp. 135, 136

130 L. D. Weatherhead, *Essays on Prayer*, A. W. Tozer & others, IVP, 1973, p. 66

131 *The Way of an Intercessor*, A. Merwood, Kingsway, 1985, pp. 74, 75

132 *Practical Prayer*, D. Prime, Hodder & Stoughton, 1985, p. 39

133 *Prayer: Key to Revival*, P. Y. Cho, Word, 1984, p. 23

134 *Standing in the Gap*, K. Gardiner, Kingsway, 1985, p. 61

135 *Born for Battle*, R. A. Mathews, OMF, 1978, pp. 38, 179

136 *Prayer*, O. Hallesby, IVF, 1948, p. 10

137 *Celebration of Discipline*, R. Foster, Hodder & Stoughton, 1980, p. 30

138 *The Meaning of Prayer*, H. E. Fosdick, Collins, 1915, p. 78

139 *Learning to Pray*, E. Pilkington, Darton Longman Todd, 1986, pp. 4, 5

140 *The Meaning of Prayer*, H. E. Fosdick, Collins, 1915, p. 72

141 *Contemplative Prayer*, S. C. Hughson, SPCK, p. 185

142 *Man, God & Prayer*, H. Northcott, SPCK, 1954, pp. 113

143 *Praying Together*, R. Rinker, Zondervan, 1968, p. 69

144 *Man, God & Prayer*, H. Northcott, SPCK, 1954, p. 196

145 *The Way of an Intercessor*, A. Merwood, Kingsway,

1985, p. 73

146 *Power in Preaching*, W. E. Sangster, Epworth, 1958, p. 105

147 *Till Armageddon*, B. Graham, Hodder & Stoughton, 1981, p. 155

148 *Prayer Power Unlimited*, J. O. Sanders, Highland Books, 1977, pp. 41, 42, 45

149 *Three Times Three Equals Twelve*, B. Mills, Kingsway, 1968, pp. 166, 167

SOURCES

The compiler thanks all authors and publishers who gave permission for quotations in this book. While every effort has been made to trace copyright holders, and ascribe quotations correctly, if there should be any error or omission, the publishers will be pleased to rectify this at the first opportunity.